Poetic Thoughts &

MEDITATIONS

for the Soul

VOL. I

JOY LaVERN OSBORNE

JOY inkz

Graphic Design, Printing
& Publishing
Crockett, CA 94525

Published By:

JOY
inkz

Graphic Design, Printing & Publishing
701 Pomona Avenue
Crockett, CA 94525

DEDICATION

To my Daddy God, my Creator, who loves me despite my imperfections.
For being my One and Only, who saves me from myself,
with your unconditional love and unmerited grace.
I dedicate this work back to you, for without your inspiration,
my pen withers to ruin.

To those whose valley experiences have consumed their lives,
I dedicate these words to renew your mind, heal your heart, and nourish your soul.

CONTENTS

ACKNOWLEDGMENTS

Thank you...

Brenton, Bryson & Braelyn, for fighting for your dreams and destiny. I love you with all I am.

Penny & Mark for true friendship and support. For being an example of living by faith and staying closer than close in my darkest hour, embracing me with the love of God.

Rhonda (Medgar) for 40+ years of showing me how to overcome and live victoriously

Gwendolyn Price for trusting my process and being the best god mom a girl could have!

Anna H. & Téné for being there when no one else could see me

Pastor LaRhonda (RHM) for being a transparent, humble leader and always pushing me to reach my fullest potential, your unconditional love, and support of what God has deposited in me. *Special* for always being there and "walking me across the street".

Gloria (James) for being loyal, I appreciate your 'no-nonsense' lessons.

Nicole (Bodo) for remaining close and walking out God's promises

Gracie for encouragement and just letting me breathe...

Lia for her confidence & authenticity, 70s style, hearts & rainbows! *Gotta have fluff stuff...*

Tangie for her example of diligence and commitment to changing the lives of youth

Anella for always seeing a brighter side and pushing for greater in me

Tiffany & Darci for 40+ years of friendship and laughter

Pastor Perkins (NJDCRM) for being a soft place for my spirit to rest.

"My Cali-fam"/Breakfast Club for being real and a breath of fresh air when I needed it the most.

"My Parents & Tex-fam" for being an integral part of my journey for over 30yrs.

Grandmother (Bishop Grace) for your prayers and 93yrs of wisdom you allow me to glean.

GNBC for inspiring me to dig deeper and withhold nothing.

EBAV for helping me find the joy in music again!

Shantay (Midwife) for walking tall in her anointing and being unafraid to use those forceps!

And to those not mentioned by name, you know your part just the same (Mimi & "Gerald")-
Thank you for the value you've added to my life, and for the smile, my heart now paints!

Lastly, for each test, trial, nightmare, situation, circumstance, and horrific event, the prince of this realm put in motion, trying to destroy me. For without persecution, there is no purpose; without fire, there is no purity; so thank you for the pain, heartache, and crushing- *God allowed it* to catapult me directly into my *Purpose!*

~ *joybelle*

Book I

Abstract

*What we visualize is oft' times the very thread
that anchors us in the abyss.*

-joybelle

Listen ©2003
Recognized work awarded Famous Poet for 2003
(2003 Poet of the Year Medallion Recipient)

I wonder if peace
Can be heard in the wind?
With each breeze that blows,
Serenity transcends.
As adversity bows its ugly head,
Tranquility surfaces
In bountiful spools like thread –
Through the eyes of life,
Sometimes shattered and weak
Lipid pools of dread
Often drowned in deceit.

I wonder if peace
Can be heard in the wind?
Or is this a shallow shell I'm in?
Forever doomed to feel pain,
And suffer great loss
At the hands of such rain?
Maybe I can hear peace,
And if I hear, others will listen;
And if they listen, others will hear.

The Rose
©2002

Roses are formed in the valley
When being tested and tried,
Though thorns and thistles rise constantly,
It's not consumed by the fire.

When you've achieved that mountain top,
The rose has finally bloomed;
And all that you've persevered,
Has only strengthened you.

It's hard to know if you can shake
The guilt and shame of sin,
To understand that beauty fades
But not when it's within.

A Vision
©2005

I wonder if you look carefully
Would you even see at all,
The reality of this circumstance
Confusing life's duality; her ever beckoning call.

Would you see through the eyes of a martyred saint?
Could that vision be full of pain?
Remembering past woes of a wounded child left alone,
Their tears would surely shame.

Maybe you see through rose-colored glasses
Laced with deceit and mistrust- on the real,
Time seems a purposeless entity
False security masqueraded
Now destiny, your soul has jaded
Only to be discarded like a cheap thrill.

I ponder the many facets of life.
What's the cost? How can I see it?
Can I pay the price?
Is seclusion a part of this game?
Just another faceless prop
With no heart and no name?

When looking is not seeing
Seeing has no vision
Visions require life's inputs
Without which, there can be no mission.

The Green
©2020

Whene'er I need a decision to make,
There's one place I can always go,
Safe from judging and prying eyes, where clarity overflows.
I find my solace on the green
As each blade caresses my stroke;
Leading me to closer to inner peace as nature cleanses every woe.

The Heart of A Dancer
©2002

Wake up at twilight,
trekking out of bed
I glance at my slippers,
as they lure me to the shed.
Carefully I laced them up
and slipped them on,
And I could feel the atmosphere
about me seemingly grow strong.

With great anticipation
I started for the door,
As my feet glided rhythmically
across the old wooden floor.
With the shed door now behind me,
My muscles begin to grow tense-
As if they knew what was about to happen,
When my body yielded
to the wanes of the soul's pretense.

The dull and rustic aura
Pulled me into its grasp,
Wanting to thrust me forward,
Yet racing to pull me back!

Emotions rush....

The bar on the wall-
Mirrors are all around,
The image portrayed cannot deny
Time has taken its toll, but not let me down.

Yet I kept each step in motion
The beat leading and guiding,
I embraced the symphony of movement
My silhouette passion inspired-

'Til my bones ache, and my soul quiets
 and my appearance is unkempt,
At dusk, I unlace my slippers
My day spent.

Q & A ©2005
Editor's Choice Award 2005 Winner
International Library of Poetry

Is the Honor of One's Integrity
Seen in their Character?
Perhaps it's mirrored
In the view of Moral Values-
Or maybe it's spoken
In the language of Love?
But can one who's illiterate to such things
Expound on potions that evolve the soul?
I think not.
The soulish realm is one of great consequence,
Where decisions outweigh your feelings-
The heart speaks volumes,
And duty-bound works have little weight.
Knowing what is right…
Accountability is a heavy sword that
Either dismembers the dead catalyst,
Or offers regenerative fluids to the soul and spirit.
Can one be honest but untruthful?
Can one have faith but swim in doubt?
Can one claim Love, yet scorn the heart?
So many questions-
Where do you place your notch?

The Sea of Forgetfulness
©2005

Here a little, there a little
A little dab will do ya,
Hither come, thither go,
From consciousness to the soul.

Oceans of emotion sweep o'er me
As the waves pay homage to the tide,
Selling the pride of your purse
Enabling my vision to emerge.

Dinner Is Served
©2005

What is it about me,
That would cause you to think
I have no heart, just a hole to fill;

With whatever dish
You're serving as a sumptuous meal-

Monday's delicacy was a T-Bone Steak
     Painfully cut with precision to the bone,
     Smothered with strife that dripped from my plate.

Tuesday's main course was Fetucinni Devine
     Lies mangled together as oodles of noodles
     Topped with a premium sauce of deceit that was just sublime!

Wednesday, of course, was Sauteed Scampi Supreme
     Poised as giant prawns of lust, with just a lite covetous dip
     Such robust flavor added to this sinful crème.

Thursday's meal Smoked Salmon & AuGratin Potatoes
     Plucked from the weeds and aroma so sweet it sickens
     Laced with a legacy of abuse and drug woes.

Friday's menu complete Italian Surprise
     A large roll of resentment
     Served with the best bitter herbs that I could handle on the side.

Saturday's dinner was Seafood Paradise
     Crabs on a massive bed with sharp red claws,
     An infectious butter sauce over rice mixed with human spices

Sunday's menu was Soul Food from Heaven
     Mutilated pork chops, mac 'n cheese, strung with yams and greens
     Deadly peach cobbler riddled with pseudo sentiment was my final sin.

What was it about me that caused you to think
     I had no heart, just a hole to fill
With whatever *you* served to me as life's final meal?

Sticks & Stones
©2020

It's so funny how awkward we are, but not ha-ha funny in the least;
So afraid to embrace our differences, we behave oft' time like beasts!
Clawing and scratching, and ohh… the wailing, from such pain we willingly inflict,
All because we're too proud and ashamed of our own shortcomings to admit.

Yeah, I saw that picture of you back in the day, with that gap between your teeth;
Sticks & Stones made you believe no one would ever take you seriously!
So you got it filled in…
I thought it was cool and loved the way it changed your words expression,
And that smile just seemed to ignite a room- purely effervescent!

Your rich, dark chocolate skin-tone, just accentuated those high cheekbones-
Yet *Sticks & Stones* snarled, your color somehow made you "illiterate" prone-
So, you set out to lighten…
What?! Like a beautiful statue, you stood, awesome in your own right,
Such power and inner wealth exuded humility in the strength of night.

Even your 'fro, so pristine and manicured, edged with perfection at the nape,
Sticks & Stones said, "too ethnic," while they served their cultures' on our plate!
So you settled…
That boy I once knew, throwing caution to the wind like feeding the ducks-
Afro, Flat-top, High Ball Fade, and even Dreads, are just expressions of trust…
     In Our Creator.
     In Our Ancestors.
     In Our Culture.
When did you create me? How do you know what makes my heart sing?
It's funny, but not ha-ha funny in the least that I gave you such power over me-
I never challenged the *Sticks & Stones'* rants or stood firmly against their plans,
Because I wasn't strong enough in my faith and the conviction of who I am-
But now, I finally get it. No matter how much I change for *"The Sticks & Stones,"*
they will never really accept me.
But why not?
Q: If you had to change for *them* to accept you, then who are *they* really accepting?
A: The "idea" of who *they* want you to be.
Q: But don't *they* expect you to accept *them* just as *they* are?
A: Yes.
Moral:
Although *Sticks & Stones* cut and break bones, they can even leave you disfigured,
Words can dismantle and destroy your life if your love of self is not bigger.
Every flavor of creation has a purpose; take pride in being YOU…
After all, there's only one.

Metamorphosis ©2007
Editor's Choice Award 2007 Winner
International Library of Poetry

Chocolate skies
Are pouring into my soul,
Forcing tainted gems
Their facets to expose.

The flesh of Rubies, Emeralds,
Sapphires and Pearls,
Diamonds and Amethysts
Wrapped in Eternity's swirl.

I can feel Vanilla clouds
Offering fluffs of indecision;
Taunting and pushing
My thoughts into submission.

No longer treasures,
Just marrow and dust;
No matter how deeply buried,
Arise…the soul must!

Butterfly
©2020

Such a beautiful creation
Wrapped in rainbows of iridescence,
Marked by an eclectic artist's brush
Such vivid color and finesse.
Her movements like liquid silk
As she glided wistfully across the sky,
Each dip and dive exposing a new facet of beauty
The autumn leaves fight for space in the light.

With the slightest wave, she commands respect
Dancing relentlessly in the breeze,
Like the dew rests in the morning
This masterpiece flutters free!

An Unambiguous Bloom
©2019

Maybe if I smiled a little more
I would remember how peace feels,
I would bathe in her sunlight
And bask as her moonbeams' reveal-
A newness and a freshness
Like I've never known before
As the twilight breaks into dusk
A new life gives way to the morn'.

Maybe if I laughed out loud
I would remember how to be merry
I would embrace the continuity of Joy
And finally, provide my heart a sanctuary;
Where her medicinal value can thrive
As it heals every spirit that's broken
In this tranquil moment, *self* dies-
And joy is reborn and spoken!

Maybe if I danced just once
I would remember the passion within
I would worship the Father relentlessly
And in the sea of Unconditional love, I'd swim-
As the rhythm and the waves sync
Each movement spins like gold-leaf
A mighty and anointed praise shower
Like the dew… it rests just beyond dawn's eve.

Maybe, will never be
Maybe, will never do
To make this change
I need right now
Finally is the word I choose!

To gain peace, joy, and love
And the other Fruit from His tree
I fully commit to the cause of Christ
That He might bloom
Within me.

My Help
©2004

They are always laughing.
They're always poking out
    their ugly little heads.

Their talons scratch me.
The breath from their nostrils
    is like a well-kindled fire!

Even their aroma…
    stinks of dead souls,
    and dead men's bones.

But they can't harm me.
For my help…
    comes from *Him*.

The Battle
©2002

Someone touched me-
    I didn't see anyone there.

Someone caressed my soul-
    I thought no one cared.

Someone breathed into me the breath of life-
    I thought I had drowned within,

Someone paid my debt with his life-
    I thought I would die in my sin!

The Son gave…
The creation took…
Such is the struggle of Christianity.

20/20 Vision
©2019

Reflecting on the things I have seen
And embraced during this tedious journey,
Brings about a change in my perception
Of all the colors that move round about me.

The emptiness of white and the density of black
Collided on my palette of life;
Forcing me into obscurity,
Trying to remove me from my plight.

Orange was deafening, and yellow burned
As I continued to press toward The Mark,
The storm of Blue seas raged,
And the sharpness of purple pierced my heart!

Just then, with His cleansing broad strokes,
The Master Painter reminded me who I am,
And how important it is to see what He sees,
It's that Focus that strengthens your lens.

You'll see the brightness of the rainbow,
God's Promise put on display
The reality of this vibrant spectrum
Sends clarity to wash the bad strokes away!

Now I understand the warmth of Red
Like the blood, Jesus shed for my sins,
He died on that rustic brown cross,
Forever making way for us to live with Him!
He is the Creator and the True Vine
And we are His branches and seeds,
Green with freshness and newness of life,
Watered by His love everlasting.

So this artist is no longer subdued by struggle or chaos,
For they are simply a means to an end,
After all, as long as Christ is my center
I have 20/20 vision
And with that… they can see Him!

Seasons
©2019

When I survey my life,
There is absolutely no doubt
Every facet of God's creation,
Carefully crafted and thought out.

Lillies Spring forth by the millions
And daffodils dance in the breeze,
While freedom blooms its lofty tune
In melodious bountiful seeds;
Lakes and streams offer to quench
Summer's drought on the wilderness plains,
Mirrored lifestyles, wandering and wanting
An everlasting fountain to sustain.

Seasons come and seasons go,
Inclement weather, storms in the Fall.
Even as autumn leaves descend,
His matchless grace still catches them all.

The Winter grips and settles in,
As icy winds bellow across the narrow road;
Keeping that anointed fire kindled
Is the only way to break the old mold-
Of discouragement and worry that contend
To keep us well beneath our concession,
So we can focus on our feelings
And not the Umbrella, for the Rain's confession!

You see, to enjoy the sunshine
We must experience the torrential rain,
Understand why it is necessary,
But most importantly, discover why we must experience pain.
As God's creation, a peculiar people,
We only sojourn through this life;
We are not here to stay, so we pray,
"Savior, please do not pass me by!
Release the bitter cold memories
Yank me from sin that soothes lusts urge,
As I Run to that Spring, that Everlasting Fountain
And embrace each season's bounty, unfettered!"

Confession
©2016

I have a friend who can write a smile upon my face
Despite all my pain,
I know someone who cared enough to die-
His death brought greater gain.

Will I ever touch the moon and the stars? Hold the sun out in my hand?
Count the grains of sand that surround the Sahara's terrain?
Maybe just balance each teardrop before it storms from the sky;
Or just consume my daily breath that only God supplied.

I can do all things through Christ because I am His own
Flesh and blood, willing and blessed, saved to the bone.
Can I dream the dreams and never grow old?
Can I walk upon those heavenly streets of gold?
I can do anything. You can be everything
We can- with God on our side, all things are possible.

That Place Over There
©2007

No matter how long it takes- I'm going to make it
No difference, whoever may stray- I'm going to make it.

No time to check the clock; it's never going to stop
Until the race is won, then I've just begun…
To see the glory on His face, I'll be happy and blessed-
In that place over there.

Though trials I may face- I'm going to make it
Misunderstood, sometimes disgraced- I'm going to make it.

Even in the valley's peak, I allow the Spirit to speak;
For the work is too great, God's Kingdom can't wait…
I'll feel the angels anointed wings, and I'll hear the heavenly hosts sing;
Worshipping at the Masters' feet, basking in His effervescent glory-
Overthere…

Replica
©2003

Wanting to leave you,
Nothing to cleave to-
You never left my side,
Though pools of tears, I cried.

The pain and hurt go deeper still,
Ever erupting within;
A lifestyle shackled
By the darkness of sin.

I can't go on,
I can't finish this day-
Forget about family
They don't care anyway;

I can't go on,
I can't finish another breath-
Too many hurts,
Not enough FAITH!

Even in my hours of despair,
I still hear your voice so fair;
Calling me, telling me, *'My love is still real*
To supply all the FAITH you need to be healed.

Remember the yesterday's I bore for you
Hold on to the hope I've birthed in you
Grasp firm the foundation I laid for you
Because you are what I made you.

A creation…
            unique and peculiar
A sensitive being…
            Your demeanor unusual, not so familiar
To my Father…
            whose image you replicate
You're made…
by the maker of whom all originate!'

Book II

Balancing Reality

It's the inhale and exhale that reminds us-
No matter the who, what, when, why, or how- we exist!

-joybelle

The Pain Is In My Eyes…
Can't You See?
©2003

How wonderful it would be
If I always knew just what to say
When you were hurting, or just down;
To brighten up your day,
And make a smile out of a frown.

What I wouldn't give to be that one,
Who is sensitive enough to realize
Exactly what you need at any given time.
But it seems my words are scarce these days,
Lifeless and meaningless sounds to say.

I'm caught in this web of what? I don't know.
But it hurts to feel love and not be able to show.
My world seems so obsolete from yours-
Unpredictability and unknowns cloud my days;
Fear of the past revealing its loathsome core,
Stormy nights often come to stay.

Mistakes created skepticism,
Love gave both joy and sorrow;
Failures caused isolation,
Life brought pain on the 'morrow.
The pain that I feel is buried so very deep,
It seems to consume the love I feel;
Can there ever be restoration?
A complete renewing of my shattered will?

I want so desperately to be like the Virtuous Woman,
Knowing what she wants and is expected of her.
But depression and broken dreams
Overwhelm me so— my vision is blurred.

What is this pain in my eyes?
Can't you see?
Not me…

Guilty Persuasion
©2008

The tears I've cried
For each lonely night
Created an Unforgiving Sea;
Too weak to leave, powerless to fight
Such bondage weighed on me.

The wounds of hurts
From years gone by
Rip open at the very seams,
Never again to heal the shame;
Of a soul-tie burdened flame.

Guilty of love in the first degree,
Guilty of peace unshackled,
Guilty of joy spontaneous and free-
His guilty persuasion is me.

Around my neck
A noose of lies
Strangled the life from me,
Little eyes so eager to learn
See cycles of hurt,
Not patience and her perfect turn.

How did this rhapsody
Swallow me whole,
Threatening my little sheep's steps?
Forgiveness is the raft
That kept me from drowning,
Lifting my head, above the seas crowning!

Guilty of hope honest and true,
Guilty of unmerited grace,
Guilty of new mercies each day I see-
His guilty persuasion is me.

Journey
©2020

Can pain ever speak
Like a blubbering fool,
Constantly jibbering
Of past woes… never living?

Can death ever grow
Like a thorny rose,
Budding and blooming,
To present peace… never forgiving?

Can hope ever dance
Like a single feather in the wind,
Floating and spinning
For future joy?

Never forgetting…
The pain
The struggle
The journey.

A Choice
©2020

What do you know about tomorrow?
What do you wish you could attain?
How do you go through life and borrow,
Never wanting to pay your way?

Although it may seem things are so easily achieved,
They only come to pass when you pay the price.
Everyone has a choice, and that's the way we were designed
So chose this day, which you hold divine.

Although your life may be full of disappointments
Chaos may rule your every thought,
But if you just take the time and listen
With an open heart, you'll find every answer you've sought.

The Bones
©2006

Day has come and time is far spent,
Joy was as bleak and desolate
As a deer in the winter snow-
Searching for a brook from which to drink.

Calmly the night releases to the Son its obsession,
Owning all, filling all who walk within his shadow
Piercing clouded eyes, dark hearts with love
Covering generations without objection.

From a particular hill at the peak of each day
In the suns rarest light
A picturesque scene of memories faded but not gone,
Such an abstract vision of royalty lay.

When the color of darkness falls like a cloak
Remember those bones that yet live,
Transfused to you and me daily
Exudes the power to destroy every yoke!

He
©2003

He can turn the tides
        and calm the sea.
He alone decides
        who writes a symphony.
He lights every star
        that makes our darkness bright,
He's forever watching
        all through each lonely night.
He finds the time to hear
        a child's first prayer,
Saint or sinner can call,
        he'll always meet them there;
Though it makes him sad to see the way we live,
He'll always say those loving words, "I Forgive."

Games
©2006

Life is about ups and downs,
It doesn't just smile; it frequently frowns.
Life can be the best, yet it can the worst
Why do we waste our time playing games?

A man and woman joined together for life
So many promises from husband to wife.
Until the vision is gone, and one is alone
Why do we waste our time playing games?

You gave everything you had, but it wasn't enough.
Trying hard to please him, but his heart was too tough.
I can't live for you, nor you for me
Why do we waste our time playing games?

Games are meant to be played by those who know the rules,
Not by those acting like fools.
For their hearts are only full of folly,
Not the unconditional love which springs eternal,
No matter the roll of the die.

Day to Day
©2002

Learn. To reach the masses through the daily dying of oneself.
Earn.   The right to choose God's way because each day, your cross will tell.

Are you driven to serve two masters? Deceived by covetous ways?
Are there so many things you cannot understand?
God already knows this; that's why He gave us His grace.

Just Do It.
Fight the good fight– of faith.
    With the sword of the Spirit– in hand
    Battle with your armor– day-to-day
    And know with God, all things He commands.

Cloak & Dagger
©2006

A game we all play,
Whether or not we want to
It's all a part of life,
When we have the ability to choose.
We are born into sin and shaped in unrighteousness
So it's effortless to live this life continually becoming more callous.
Concerned about yourself, how you feel and what you want
The needs of others are non-existent in your world of bondage.

Even the milestone that hangs around your neck is there by choice,
To admit there is a milestone, you would have to yield to God's voice;
Without His eyes, you only see what you think you want- not what's for you.
Before you accept Jesus into your heart, your vision cannot improve.
So really, you do not see at all,
You're being distracted by the enemy's decoy,
Because he knows if your focus is distorted,
He can get you to forfeit your joy!

You see, on his own, he can't win; his fate is absolute;
He relies on secrets and undercover dealings to keep your praise on MUTE.
After all, why would you praise or pray to a God you can't see,
Well, the chains that bind you are just as vivid- are you asking the enemy for a key?
The lies you told, the things you stole, the pain you inflicted on the weak-
The drugs you took, even those dirty books, are all different links!
Maybe sleeping around and being ornery is the lifestyle you choose
Continuing to disobey the laws of the land puts your neck in a noose.

Although Cloak & Dagger will always be a choice of perspectives,
We choose to let our spiritual eyes give us the clarity by which to live.
Our cloak is the garment of praise that covers the spirit of heaviness;
So regardless of how you feel, when you offer true worship, you're blessed!
The dagger is the sword of the spirit, which is the Word of God;
It's priceless and will never pass away, so it can never, ever be lost!

With my cloak on my back and my dagger at my waist,
I invite humility, courage, and faith-
That Jesus' blood would forever cleanse
And sin no longer abide,
And my vision of victory crystal clear
As I now walk with Christ!

Battle Scars
©2017

Remember, we are all in a war...

> Our physical scars remind us-
> > where we have been and what we have endured.
> Our emotional wounds keep us
> > broken and humble before a Mighty God.

Each of our testimonies is unique so that no one can express your journey like you. The battle is learning from your past and making those choices that bring about a life change. After all, you wear the scars that prove you have already gone through it;

> So STAND TALL and set someone else free,
> By honoring God's Word and reminding us all-
> > *"We are set free by the blood of the Lamb*
> > *and the words of our testimony." (Romans 12:11)*

Bait & Switch
©2018

The "called" submitted and was chosen,
What's done by the spirit is clear;
No matter the words that were spoken,
The works bore fruit that was lived!

I choose to speak over my seeds,
Not as they are now- but what they have already become;
My life, sold out, as a faithful steward of the Highest,
Has transformed my harvest in the Son.

You see, it's one thing to hear,
And another to heed and discern;
My self-worth is my *Joy*, not my job;
A lesson the enemy wished that I had never learned!

The devil is the one who's just done,
It's a fate that he cannot escape;
My treasures may seem nil in your eyes,
But in the hands of the Master, they're Great!

A Cartoon *(Blip)*
©2020

I don't remember what happened; let me just make one thing clear,
It's going to sound absurd when I tell you what I hear.
It all started before I was formed, just a twinkle in my mother's eye;
Nine months later, thanks to the Creator,
Bright, with ultimate lung capacity, I arrived.
A little splotch here, *Blip*- Lots of sounds, animated gestures, and blinks
A little dab there, *Blip*- Expressions, without words; as if they were ever linked
My language and my sounds were melded together like a grilled cheese sandwich,
And some kind of way my method of expression made an entirely new game of it!

You see, whenever something would happen, no matter if it was bad or good;
I could hear the sound effects blastin' so loud that my ears shook!
It's like my mind took pictures of what the sounds should be,
So when things would actually happen, I would be tickled immensely!
POW! ZAP! ZOOM! BANG! *Blip* Just a few that caught my attention-
BLURP! ZOWWIE! ARGHHH! BUFFF! *Blip*. The sound for me, in my opinion,
        was as necessary as breathing and a part of me like skin.
Even when I saw some foods move around my plate,
The sounds of ocean waters or bubbling brooks determined my stomach's fate!

I didn't realize until much later; I didn't know how to live
I went through life just absorbing things, not understanding I was the *Blip*!
Not the meat of a movie that grabs you quick and nestles you in its plot;
Not the vegetable of a commercial, that gives you quick nutrients on the spot.
Not even the dessert of the news that satisfies the need for knowledge,
But that *Blip* of a cartoon you swore had zero substance and was as good as garbage…
        Sometimes on mute *(sound effects are crucial, they'll help you get the gist)*-
        Tom & Jerry, friends and adversaries depending on the day;
        They both reveled in exciting anecdotes that tickled me when I played.
        Fred was loud and bossy too; his best friend Barney on the Flintstones
        Wilma & Betty, both firm and the glue to these two rebels getting along.
        Huckleberry Hound blast from the past; he danced and sang all the time-
        He was blue, wore a hat, and sang about his Darling Clementine!
        Pixie, Dixie continually trying to outsmart their nemesis, Mr. Jinks
        Snaggle Puss, Yogi Bear, and Touché the Turtle all enjoyed the finer things,
        They were heroes, creative thespian mentors I saw in my dreams.

Each of my cartoons was family, providing such humor and happiness for me
Their nonsensical way seemed to lift my spirit of laughter, unapologetically.
Just a commercial in this program of life I'm not…
A *Blip*, a cartoon, the perfect thought!

Clean Out The Clutter
©2006

I can't seem to breakthrough
These walls of misery,
Because I've got so much stuff,
It's hard for me to see.

All I want is not what I need,
To fulfill a purpose- my destiny.
He said I needed to clean out the clutter of my life.

Behind closed doors,
there are so many wars;
Skeletons of the past
Fight for life behind the mask.
Closets bursting, seams splitting within
The masquerade is over contention now, my closest friend.

So many things I want to keep:
Trinkets and memories, oh so sweet;
But having too much weighs me down,
I cannot feel your warmth on my brow.

If all I want is not what I need,
Break me and shape me in my destiny-
And help me clean out the clutter of my life!

God cannot lie-
What He says is what He'll do;
On His Word, I can depend,
Regardless of what I've been through.
He carries me in my darkest hour,
When I have no power to stand
My sins washed away
In the sea of Forgetfulness,
As only His blood can!

He said He would clean out the clutter,
And all He would recover;
Soon I would discover,
His love is like no other
He cleaned out the gutter of my life!

Truth
©2005

Does the grass grow greener
on the other side?

Fallen tears,
heightened fears
Overshadowed by a past
       that I cannot
       seem to *bear.*

Where does the ocean
flow into the sea?

Wounds so deep,
cuts that bleed
Cast aside,
       forgotten by those
       who seemed to *care.*

Does the sky ever end…
       after you've climbed the clouds?

I've lost faith in the one
who sacrificed His Son
Finding it so very hard
       to cleave to
       the UNSEEN *one.*

Does the end of the rainbow
hold my destiny?

All my guilt and shame
I carry are my cross
Though burdened and heavy laden
       you paid my debt
       and *WE WON!*

Secure Your Vision
©2018

Stay out of your own way,
Get out of your own head,
Be relentless about Kingdom building,
And only say what God says!

For all else will pass away,
Heaven, earth, you and I;
But the unadulterated Word of God is the key to Living-
Beyond when you die.

So eat from the pages of the script
He lived and left for us to glean,
He's the only God who created this masterpiece-
The human form so complex and redeemed!

Take the time to talk to him daily
And make sure you get rid of any weeds,
You cannot focus if you cannot see
And with no vision- you perish inevitably!

Careful for Thee
©2011

I will give
My all to you
No matter what it takes,
I will not hold back
Anything if only
you would make-

Me whole again
Useful in your hands
Deserving of your love
Worthy of your plan;
For my life, in its complexity
Is so care-filled
I forgot I must be
Careful for thee.

A Path To Healing
©2006

For every tongue that was used to
Assassinate my character, curse, and lie;
I choose to speak God's blessings
Over every part of your life.

For every action that was taken
To try and break me and sabotage my walk;
I choose for God's love to reign down
And cover all your hurting thoughts.

You see, in the end, I can only thank you...
Although a tool you might have been,
Sandpaper is what you actually were;
That shines and buffs this diamond,
So His purpose will not be detoured!
But do not be dismayed, even the tool can be redeemed and live,
Just repent, embrace God's love, and let His blood cover and forgive! (I Peter 3:9-14)

I Am...
©2009

It's not fair that others have what I want,
And they don't even have to try;
It's not right for the rich to get richer
And not even bat an eye.

Why can't I have it all?
Why not me?

You can— just know I'm the maker of wine...
That quenches the thirst for eternity
The Creator of all that breathe life
I am who I am, I am the Christ.

Lord, I'm thankful to be chosen
Just to be worthy of your pain;
To endure these tests and trials
And count it all joy in the end.

One-Touch
©2011

Can I touch you, Lord?
Can I feel the warmth of your love?
Can I see your fire from above?
Can I smell your fragrance so sweet,
Can I hear your Spirit speak?
Can you cradle me in your arms?
Can you shelter me from the storm?
Can you heal my broken heart?
Can you give me a brand new start?

'Yes. You can touch me.
But will you let me touch you?
I promise if you just surrender and call Jesus' name
You will never, ever be the same!'

Is it enough to want to be pure? Is it enough to want to feel secure?

'No! You've got to take the next step and repent of your sins-
Then I can come and sup with you and abide within
I'll change your life and give you hope,
Drown your sins in the Sea of Forgetfulness,
To remember them no more!'

I repent of my sins and turn to you.
Jesus, are you there? Can I touch you?

He touched me.
I'm not sure what happened, but I feel refreshed!
For the first time in a long time, my spirit is at rest.
Jesus, I now know you live in me
Thank you for sending your son to die on that tree.
I can live, and I'm ready to move on,
Now that all the emptiness is gone.
Even my presence seems to glow,
As others express the change they see,
I know it must be my soul!
Finally, in sync with my maker
I'm on my way to bigger and better.
Without you, I would still be dust
It was so simple, and it just took one touch.

Hideaway
©2011

Honestly-

Do you think you can fool me?
  The One who before the foundations of the world spoke, and there was?
  The One who masterfully created each being as a unique entity?
  The One, born of a virgin, teacher of priests, doer of miracles?
  The same One unjustly accused and crucified for the sins of the world?

And you still think...
  You can hide your sins within your DNA?
    (which I authenticated before you were a whisper)
  Your religiosity, ideologies, and theologies can cover your sins?
  You can tuck your indiscretions behind the mask of magnanimous living?
  Your flowery words, coated with pseudo-pleasantries, can mask the heart's intent?

No.
Just Tell the Truth.
Receive the Truth- Me!

I am GOD...
  Before me, there was none-
  And after me, there can be no other.
I am...
  Omnipotent, Omniscient and Omnipresent one.
I am...
  Time, and the Authority over life, death, and the grave.
I am...
  The same One who hears the blood from your sins crying out for me!
I am...
  The same yesterday, today, and forever!

So think again.

There's no place to hide.

Repent.
And Turn...
Pride cometh before the fall...

Never Forget To Remember
©2018

When I think of the goodness of Jesus,
And all that He's done for me,
I remember...

The many days that were so dark,
I did not think I would ever see the light again;
But just then,
        He cried for me.

Bound by circumstance, loss, and grief
The burden was almost too much to bear;
Just then,
        With nails in His hands,
        He set me free.

When corrupt thoughts and actions consumed my being,
To snuff out the very word of my testimony;
Just then,
        He was wounded
        for my transgressions.

So many times, I've not only fallen but walked away,
Giving in to my fleshly desires;
But just then,
        He was bruised
        for my iniquity.

Even when I stumbled through the valley of the shadow of death,
And fear tried to strangle the very life from my soul,
Just then,
        The chastisement
        of my peace was upon Him.

He gave up 'the ghost,' and His work was finished,
My soul cries out, "Hallelujah,
Praise God for saving me!"
For by his stripes I am healed,
And I will never forget to remember-
The inheritance that Jesus' blood sealed.

Book III

Out of the Darkness

Even in the darkest of nights, there remains a Light that shines brighter still;
Guiding you through the wilderness of pain to a safe harbor to rebuild.

-joybelle

Someone Like Me
©2002

If I thought it really mattered,
How I looked today
Like a bag lady searching for a dream;
I would have been proud,
    to be my own crowd
      In an oversized shirt and Queen jeans.

But the norm doesn't pay
By the size that you weigh
They only want to hurt your pride–
They can't understand,
    Just a frame I am
      Of a picture being painted on the easel of life.

The ocean is vast as the deep blue sea,
So it doesn't matter
what you say about me;
Flowers still bloom, and birds still sing
So what's wrong with loving someone like me?

I'm a big girl with big dreams filling my head
It's kicking and tearing me apart-
But these feelings won't last,
    a few days will pass
      and a new life will become my heart.

When the roses turn red
And violets turn blue,
The XXX's and Queen's
Have paid their dues-
    we will be dancing
      in the pure sunlight;

The angels,
    mother nature,
    my baby
    and I…

Soul Tie
©2003

The object of my affection
A soul-tie connection.

I thought you taught me about love yesterday
How to be complete in any and every way,
Only demons of the past were brought to fruition
Laying to rest a once sure foundation;
Trusting you was all that I needed,
Never realizing you were not yet seasoned–
For me, this time in space will be void
As I grasp at tangibles to silence the noise.
Orchids, Tiffany's– all necessary tools,
They tell of *Victoria's Secrets*, not a whispering fool.

But yesterday is gone and today is tomorrow
The strengths I once knew are now drowned in sorrow.
For the mirror reveals pain, hurt and self-degradation
These the lasting effects of a self-absorbed relation.

Though from this, three bright lights ever shine
Proving that good can always penetrate the darkest of times.
Is our time finished? Is our journey complete?
The answer illuminates as my breath escapes quickly–
Love doesn't walk on eggshells,
Or demand itself as payment for life's pressures stilled.

The choice to choose is yours this day
Love me completely or just walk away,
No need for pretending all is well;
The scars run too deep, erupting in pure hell.

Deserving of a crown, and perfect, not me;
But embraced like the gift, that was sent to be–
Respected and loved and treated like your Queen.
Not sexed with an erection of lust,
Crushed beneath words and deeds of mistrust.
Undeniably coveted, unconsumed by spirituality's dove
Forever changing my song,
Silencing my melody in the key of Love.

Unbreakable
©2020

Do you care that I'm hurting today?
So much so, I feel torn in two.
The words that you didn't say
The call that you didn't make-
    was all I thought I needed
     to make it through.

You say you love me for who I am
But can't respect who I want to be.
By trying to hinder this master plan
It only makes me surely STAND-
    on the stage of my purpose
    and destiny.

Everlasting, reassuring, and true;
And liberating hope always so fresh
I find life blossoms when I pursue
Those things by design I do
    with joy,
     clarity and finesse.

So I understand now your goal
The easiest way to escape
To break and shatter this mold
Preventing my roots from growth
    an upgrade of morality
     you just couldn't fake it!

Now that my resolve
    has settled the storm
    I bid farewell to you
    My heart is no longer forlorn-

For the cost of its passions past due
    was the expression
    of love
    in creativity
    a New!

What Do You Want?
©2004

What do you want me to do?
  Perhaps cool my jets and dumb myself down
  Or maybe even throw caution to the wind.
  I'm so torn with such emotion in the state I'm in.
What do you want me to do?
  Perhaps just pray for a little while
  Or maybe just sit and listen
  And maybe I'll grasp some divine wisdom.
What do you want me to do?
  Perhaps I shouldn't think at all
  Maybe it's just another trick for blind eyes to see
  Or perhaps it's not, but just something else to bind me.

 Such is the battle in the mind from day today
 It's hard to figure out just what to do or say-

I know what I want...
  To LIVE life to the fullest and have good laughs
  To enjoy each other's company and stroll down moonlit paths
  To honor and respect this sacred intimacy from above
  To never ask for more than I'm willing to give and embrace this love.
I know what I want...
  To support your dreams and push your purpose in everything with you
  To be authentically ME, as no one else could ever do!
  To be BOLD, HONEST, QUICK WIT and SASSY
  These traits are what make my joy completely creatively CLASSY!
I know what I want...
  To know you will always give yourself to me
  A touch, a pat, a caress-withholding no secrets or schemes.
  You want what I want, and we've both had time to heal,
  Now we must face life together, with the 3-fold chord to keep us yielded.

What exactly is it that you want me to do?
  Give in... I can't. The cost is too great!
  Play games...I won't. For too long, I've had to wait.
  Respect you... I must, For choosing to stand by my side.
  Love you... I will. For in Him, our love abides.
  Honor you... I will. Because you know the stories end.
  Adore you... Always. In you, I'll forever have a friend.

I Choose?
©2007

It's the same; nothing has changed
Looking in a mirror,
    don't like what I see
A woman full of pain
    and oh, such misery!

Down and out,
Masquerading in a world
    full of doubt.
Bills due, money few,
    can't seem to pay my way
Kids cryin', nerves tryin'-
    I'm on the verge
    of losing my faith.

I thought I could love
    without you,
I didn't realize
    I couldn't make it through;
But because of your grace
    and mercy I can stand,
I've weathered the storm
    because I held your hand.

Now I'm full,
    so satisfied and filled with such joy;
My life and my trust in you
    has blocked the noise-
Of the enemy
    who once shackled my mind,
But now I'm free
    and You have redeemed the time!

You picked me up when I was down
You made things right,
    the smile I now wear
was once a frown.

There's no life without you,
The only new beginning
    is the one that I choose!

Out of Your Mind
©2002

Did you think that I
Would love you unconditionally?
Without any of your lovin'
Reachin' out to me?
I can't understand
How a so-called man
Could love you and leave,
And steal the air that you breathe.

You were out of your mind
To make believe we were fine,
To hold me at night
Like everything was alright.
Then you turned and walked out
And left my heart in the clouds
I can't forget—all that I gave
For all of your doubts.

Maybe this love,
        was doomed from the start
And maybe my eyes
        were seeing through your heart.
If love wasn't meant to hurt,
        then I did it all wrong
I gave all I had to give
    But you didn't want my part.

Forever I thought I'd love you,
Never we'd be apart-
I could never have imagined
This loveless heart.

Now that I see clearly
What loving you means,
I'd rather be alone
Than with you hurtin' me!

Broken Promises
©2004

Times were rough, and times were hard
When we started this love, we knew we'd go far
But one day you stopped givin',
and I refused to keep livin'
And being torn apart.

How could you go, after all, we've been through
How could you leave, with a child and one due;
I don't understand how your heart's not made of stone?
You promised your love, but now we're alone.

It's finally over, but there's no time to breathe
I've gotta keep it together because I know these little eyes see-
A broken, hurt woman, trying to find her way
Fighting with everything she has to see a brighter day!

I can't even blame you for all the mistakes that were made
We were young and had the baggage we collected along the way.
After a while, there was no room for anything else,
So something had to give, and I put my feelings on the shelf.

I see that you're talkin' 'bout coming back around;
But I'm not that same simple girl that you so long ago found;
I've been through the storm, survived the flood;
You have to give of yourself to be loved.

And if you don't love yourself, it will not work out for your good-
You must embrace your journey- all your mistakes, the happy & misunderstood;
Even those things that were done to violate your trust
For through such darkness, a rose springeth forth, as forgiveness whispers *"Hush."*

It's not the fact that you didn't care
    or even want to work things out…
It's that you simply made a promise
    but shifted the burden when there was doubt.

You didn't trust yourself to be there.
You couldn't lend yourself to prayer.
When your voice echoed off the walls,
You found the emptiness I had known all along.

Separate Lives
©2002

Trying to make sense
Of this love I thought was mine,
I just can't believe
It's faded with time.
All I ever wanted
Was a feeling that would last,
But I didn't realize
You were my future and past-

I couldn't give love
For the pain I felt within,
Dashed dreams and aspirations
Troubled by inner fears.
All that I had
I gave from my heart-
It wasn't enough; now we're torn apart.

We tried everything
That we knew to stay together,
But all time revealed
Were motives concealed
        to bring about inclement weather!
Poutin' and talkin,'
we both seemed to be walkin'
Separate ways–to separate lives.

If I thought peace of mind
Could be found in your arms,
I would run and embrace
Your love.

But time has taught me well,
A lesson I'll not fail
I must stay away...
And protect this rose bud.

There's no time to be bitter
The years have gone by fast
The truth in memories garden
Is to learn how to embrace the past!

There's Only One Me
©2002

Who are you foolin' in this game of life,
You'd think I'd know by now– 'cause I am your wife.
You told me forever when it could never be,
You'd never say it, so I'm tellin' you to leave.

Go on down to the ocean painted blue,
Listen to the seashells and the mermaids too;
They'll say there's other fish in the sea,
But ain't no pretendin' – there's only one me.

You came in at 4 AM after partyin' all nite,
You drank it up with the boys, and now you wanna fight;
I ain't got no reason to indulge your mood-
Where's the man I married, 'cause it sure isn't you.

Run to the river with green-tinted beads,
Playback the songs from the willowing reeds;
You'll see a lot of fish that appear to swim free,
But ain't no pretendin' – there's only one me.

A stride is a stride in this walk of life,
When push comes to shove, there's just no more love;
No need to be angry, no need to shout,
Now you've got plenty of time just to hang out.

Rest by the lake rich with the earth,
While the breeze whistles a tune of nature's first.
No matter the fish, you must still carry its weight;
No pretense,
No excuses,
But this time, use the REAL bait.

Not to duplicate the experience of the decoy
But if you give more of yourself,
You'll get back more joy;
And although this fish
Has found an ocean within,
It's never too late
To help a fellow traveler to win!

I Cross My Heart
©2015

I crossed my heart
    and hoped to die
    'twas a foolish
    childish cry;
Flesh to flesh,
    a man's life
    I did not know
    the cross was mine.

Then one day
    I heard of "The Man,"
    who carried the weight
    of the world
    and my guilty stains;
He nailed them all
to an old wooden cross,
    high on a hill
    His pain and anguish-
    My sins debt
    fulfilled.

I cross my heart
    and hope to die
    to heal this hurt,
    this shattered life;
I cross my heart,
    I want to live
    for I could never
    take more than
    You give.

I cross my heart
    and hope to die
    to kill this flesh
    and sinful pride–
I crossed my heart
    with Jesus' blood
    forever cleansed,
      I can't give up.

My Father's Heart
©2019

There's something I need to see,
Someone I need to become;
The answer lies in you,
No place to hide from the Son.

A life so full yet empty-
Where can I run but to you Lord?
The bondage of religion and busyness,
Has changed your voice to muffled noise...

But the yearning within my soul,
Outweighs the breaking of my heart
As I search for the door
To my Father's heart.

So I humbly served and offered my gifts,
Sacrificing the true me
Conformity, the new wave of surrender,
It all just seemed too easy.

In the end there's *A Battle Cry*
Of The Shadow of My Father's Heartbeat
It restored my broken vessel,
Proving a warrior yet worthy.

The yearning within my soul,
Outweighs the breaking of my heart
As I search for the door
To my Father's heart-

He says...'I'm still here, where you left me
I didn't change the lock or code to the door,
Faith's the only key you've ever needed
Won't you please just talk to me, once more?

The path to the heart of THE FATHER, is just beyond your pain
Over the hills of fear, and through the storm and rain;
You can never be too far, because He's never left your side
It is He who is God and only in Him, does true love abide'.

Intimacy's Cost
©2017

Often I ponder,
On the things of my past,
Wondering if things were different,
Maybe fewer scars I'd have;
But it doesn't change the person,
God created me to be
All the pain, hurt, and shame
      only killed
      the flesh of me.

Each day,
I die a little more
To be like Jesus is a priceless journey
That presses more fresh oil;
But please never mind the cost,
The debt has already been paid
His blood- covered my sin;
      conquered hell
      and the grave.

This work is too great,
So I cannot come down
No matter how deep the valley
To Jehovah Nissi's banner, I'm bound.
Though all may forsake me,
I shall not retreat
Your Word is- working intimacy,
      and breathing
      breath into me.

I'm knocking out these windows,
Tearing down these walls
You're refilling me with everything I need.
I'm not willing to give up,
This intimacy I have with you;
It's everything, and you're everything-
      my breath through
      and through!

Free
©2006

Save me, Lord, from myself
Hold me, Lord, I need your help
Break me, Lord– save my soul
Root out pride and make me whole.
Wipe my tears through the night
Bear my fear; it'll be alright.
Take my hand, precious Lord
Fill my cup 'til I want no more.

Guide me through this narrow way
Hold me near, and I will not stray.
I can't go on by myself
There isn't any use; I need your help!

Breathe on me and set me free
There's no other way it can be.
I've tried to do it on my own,
But I just sank deeper like a stone;

So I yield this vessel to you,
To do with as you choose.
I thank you in advance for sifting my needs,
That I can live totally and completely free!

Victory
©2007

Without your love, I don't know what I would do
Without your hope, I could not pull through;
Without your peace, I could not stand the rain
Without your grace and mercy in my life, I could not take the pain.

It's all about Jesus- the blood, the name, the power
It's only Jesus- the watcher, keeper of each hour
It began with Jesus- My Creator, Savior, and Lord
It ends with Jesus- the *Victor of the War!*

When God Calls My Name
©2017

I hear you whistle in the wind,
I feel your warmth through the fingers of the sun;
I see you in the morning's dew,
New mercies just have begun…

As a new day is dawning,
Every second, minute, and hour;
My spirit feels the freshness of
Your blood's resurrection power!

When God calls my name,
It's that still small voice within;
I secure my hold to His Hand
He whispers, 'Renewed Hope and Strength!'

My opportunity to hear Him
And choose to guard my soul,
Is not easy when so many dark forces,
Torment me in their battle for control.

But yet He says, 'Come unto me;
Bring your burdens and your pain,
Your heartaches and your suffering,
For in Me, there's only gain.

I loved you enough…
> When my Only Son Jesus chose to shed
> His blood on Calvary
> I crushed the penalty of sin,
> So you'd be free- just to hear me!

I loved you still…
> When up from the grave, Jesus
> Ascended with the keys,
> The debt you owed, I paid in full
> So listen with your heartstrings!'

An Ought
©2019

The other day I pondered yesteryear
Recounting the ways satan stroked my fears,
By planting a single thought of dismay
The seed grew into an ought and would not go away!
When happiness came to my door and knocked,
That ought checked the bolt and made sure it was locked;
Not only the door but the windows were boarded up,
The chimney was blocked, and even the flute was shut!

So now all alone, just that ought and me
I realize there can be no joy if you're not free;
For although that ought pretends to shut out the pain,
What it did was held me captive, bound to the shame-
Of all the ought's before, that we're now having a convention
Playing out their roles, some with honorable mention!

I was convinced my life was expendable, not necessary to the call;
Then that old devil slipped up and made the biggest mistake of all.
As if the death threats and malleable sickness weren't enough,
He told me God did not care about any of my stuff!
After all, if He was my God and really did exist
Why such hardships and pain on me afflict?
My mind was in a tailspin as I remembered another
Whose plight was much worse, and he was not just another brother.
Job was his name, the personification of trials to a tee
Ordained and sanctioned to prove to the devil God's sovereignty.

Enough is enough, and these ought's have to go,
Because I cannot see Him if my garments are these clothes.
I must put on the garment of praise and carry heaviness no more
Be clothed in righteousness, yielding His armor and sword.
Use the weapon of prayer and consistently stay open to His voice,
Cling to His every promise for, ultimately, my destination is my choice.

So listen, do not allow an ought in your heart to abide,
For it is really the enemy's masquerade- he's taking you for a ride!
Never give satan a foothold of any measure
He will use whomever he can to gain power for his pleasure.
Remember when life happens, people chatter, and chaos can ensue
Keep clean hands and a pure heart, and rest in His holy 'ought-free' residue!

(*NOTE: If you handle life's issues with wisdom, love, and grace
God will keep you 'ought-free' while you continue this race!)

Zion Is Calling
©2017

Though problems come
    on ever hand
And darkness
    clouds your view
Loved ones don't seem
    to understand
Those things God has
    for you to do.

Don't be dismayed,
He'll never leave your side;
For Zion is calling
You to open your eyes.

From the mountain
    I can see the valley low
Where the river of discouragement
    continuously flowed-
Pushing and pressing,
    challenging my hold
But yet and still
    there's one thing I know-
No matter how far
    away He seems
Zion is surely
    calling me.

When fear shatters
    your hopes and dreams
And pity
    replaces your joy
Situations and temptations
    will daily come
But just remember
    I've given you a choice.

Choose ye this day whom you will serve
For Zion had given you- *His Word.*

Never Lookin' Back
©2002

You said you loved me
You said you cared
But when I needed you
You were never there.

Your words meant nothing
Just a cold winters breeze
I'm better off alone
Than beggin', you do right by me.

Those little things you've done
Just for the fun of it
Ain't sittin' well with me
No, not one bit!

There just ain't no excuse
For your walkie talkie ways
I can't take it anymore
There just ain't enough days...

Gonna shake the dust
        from my boots
'Cause in a few more years
        they're gonna be roots;
Gonna leave this tired man alone
Never lookin' back,
        no matter 'bout his hat!

That hat hung around for days-
        never admittin'
I don't wanna see it no more-
        I'm not kiddin'

It stormed through my life,
And settled on a thorn;
Caused me too much pain-
Leave the hat alone!

Be Careful
©2018

Caught up in the middle of these tests and trials
Not knowing which way to turn
With problems all around me
Each day offers a new discerning plea-

Be careful of what you say and do,
Care less about the trials you go through;
For God has called for a peculiar one
To be careful, not care-filled when the day's done.

All of the pain that has consumed my soul
Does not matter at all,
Its purpose to make me a glistening testament
When through this fire, I must walk;
A midst the tormentor's venoms talk!

Glide unscathed, beneath deaths' sharp fingers,
As the Heavenly Host takes my hand
Though the scars of battle I proudly bear;
In His triumphant victory,
This diamond will share!

I'll sing Glory to God in the Highest
And my heart will leap for joy
All praises to the One true King
As I worship Him for all eternity!

So remember …
This is just a rehearsal-
Being Careful to make the right choice;
For when the battle's fought and won
I want to hear
'My good and faithful servant
Well Done!'

A New Altar
©2017

Dry bones have encamped around my altar
Their presence brought misery and strife
How can I do good,
When this evil is ever before me?
How can I be perfect in Thy sight?

Recommitting my life
I count it all joy…
Redefining my vision
I was cast down but not destroyed.

God says, 'I'll always be with you,
Don't be distressed, neither be denied;
Though persecuted, you're never forsaken-
For your foundation is the altar
For God's sacrifice.

When trouble is on every side
And confusion everywhere,
Remember, trials come only
To make you strong;
Changing your mind
Is realigning your life,
With the blueprint
I've imprinted on my own.

Just give me your broken spirit
And the sorrowful
And humble heart,
Then I will rejoice…
For this is an honorable
And worthy sacrifice.'

So, I'm consecrating the foundation f
For a new altar
To be used for sacrificial praise;
With the mortar of faith
And the brick of His Word
My altar will stand as a testament
To God's grace.

Book IV

I Wonder..?

Often the questions that we ask are symptoms of our life's condition.
Whether or not the diagnosis is correct,
Depends on the authenticity of the heart.

-joybelle

The Watchman
©2017

In the distance,
I see greener pastures,
Treasures and a wide road that seems right;
With so many travelers walking therein
Conformity pierced my side.

That thorn in my flesh
Reminded me
To stay focused on His way,
Never leaning on my own understanding,
Always cultivating that mustard seed faith.

Oh, I'll let nothing
Come between my God and me,
The tests and trials will eventually be gone.
I won't be discouraged,
Though the pathway seems bleak,
He guides my footsteps and leads me on.

Though the devil
Has tried to take my life
The battle is not His to win,
He's just a distraction to make me fall
The more I press, the stronger I ascend!

At times the hem
Seems unraveled,
You can't see through the eye of the storm;
His peace around you finds the needle,
And repairs those cords of your heart so worn.

I will not give in,
I cannot come down
For the Master has called me out.

The work is too great,
As the watchman on the wall,
I am victorious
By the hem
Of Christ's' gown.

If I Could (Be Like You)
©2016

If I could take away your pain
Erase the guilt and shame
Remove all sin and doubt
Brighten a stormy cloud
Then I would be free to be like you.

If I could heal your wounded soul
Bear your heavy load
Mend your broken heart
Give a brand new start
Then I would be free to be like you.

To be like you
I long to be like you
Always pure
Awesome and sure
I want to be like you.

Because of your blood, I can…
     Live eternally
     Set the captives free

Because of your love, I am…
     Not ashamed of your word
     I'm empowered to reach the earth
     Just like you.

Hmm…?
©2009

There are so many things I see differently than before,
And the last time I checked, I still had the same eyes;
It causes me to ponder, on a lot of the wonder-
I have experienced throughout my lifetime.

So what do I do?
I simply ask you… Will you answer?

To Be Like You
©2015

When I don't have
  It's not because
  you can't give
When I am sick
  It's not because
  you don't live
When I am blind
  It's not because
  you can't see
Oh, how I want
  To be more like Thee…

When I am hungry
  It's not because
  you can't provide
When I am lonely
  It's not because
  you can't abide
When I am burdened
  It's not because
  you can't bear

Oh, how I want
To be more like the Savior.

I want more
  than a mansion
I want more
  than silver and gold
More than
  fame or shallow thrills
Far more than
  wealth untold.

To be like you
What must I do?
Clean my heart
And wash me through and through-

I want to be…
Just like you.

It's Just Who He Is
©2010

A pain-free life
May not be promised-
        but a peaceful one is.
The feeling of loneliness
May want to linger,
        and yet His comforting touch will.

No matter the restless nights,
Nor the seemingly never-ending hopeless days,
Just remember- God Is.

He is-
The moon that…
        calms each night,
The sun that…
        brightens the sky;
The breeze that…
        calms the sea,
The dew that…
        highlights His glory.

He is also-
The storm that…
        cleanses our soul,
The droughts…
        reminiscent of the days of old;
The tornados that…
        uproot our very beings,
The hurricanes that…
        drive us to our destiny.

What?
Why?
How?
When?

All these questions,
And there can only be one answer-

He Is. GOD IS!

Just Give Me You
©2015

Question:

Who do you love…
      If love is in the sweetness
      of your words?
Who do you trust…
      If honesty is a good thought
      that collects dust?
Who do you honor and praise…
      If you can't give yourself completely
      all of your days?

Answer:

I love you.
I trust you.
I give you all.
What else can I say,
Before I turn and walk away.

Question:

Why do you run…
      When Christ is sitting on the throne?
Why do you hurt…
      When He went to Calvary all alone?
Why do you cry…
      When He covered all when He died?

Answer:

Give me your love.
Trust me with your life.
Just give me your all.

What else can I say,
Before I turn and walk away.

Reminisce
©2009

When I think about Jesus and His sacrifice,
How His blood for me at Calvary flowed;
I am reminded of the brokenness He endured,
When He paid a debt, He did not owe.

He chose to leave His heavenly home
Knowing who He was and what would be,
The entire sin of the world he would take on
Though encased in the flesh- He was Divinity's seed.

He never spoke of a burdensome regret,
Even when repeatedly asked to give more;
Though tempted by satan and despised by man,
He remained holy and righteous to the core.

For this was the plan from the beginning,
To sacrifice the holy unblemished Lamb;
Only a sinless offering could atone for my stain,
When in the sea of iniquity, I swam.

He gently held out his unwavering hand,
Beckoning me to hold fast;
To open my heart and receive Him in
Repent and turn from my wicked past.

I never knew of a love so sweet,
Unconditional and ever so sublime;
Its power can purify the darkness of nights
And transform the hearts of humankind!

That same love met me in the depths of hell
Where my soul was destined to be,
The key to the grave and power over death
He snatched when He ascended to glory.

So yes! How sweet it to think on His name
And reminisce on how Jesus' journey saved,
His blood continues to give me strength
And its power can never be erased!

A Prayer of Healing
©2008

I saw a crippled child on the corner yesterday,
The distant look in her eyes
Touched my heart in a particular way.
Although I didn't have much to say
I had a lot to give;
And I raised my hands towards heaven And
gave a prayer of healing-

I cried, "Lord touch this child
And she'll never be the same,
Cleanse her body and her mind
From all sin, guilt, and shame;
But at the same time, give her peace Beyond
all understanding,
So Lord honor this prayer of healing."

With tears in her eyes,
She softly spoke these words,
'I don't understand, and I don't know why I
feel so different than before.
The emptiness is gone, and I've got joy
Where there was despair;
Please tell me– I've got to know
What is it you've got to share.'

I said, "Child, what I have
Is more precious than silver or gold,
It can change the darkest sky
And fill it with sunny rainbows;
With every day and every hour
Your faith builds more and more-
It's just a simple prayer,
A prayer of healing.

There's a healing power
This very hour,
Just pray the sincere prayer,
And open your heart to God's care.
From heaven above, God sent His love… to
bear burdens as the Comforter.

Faith's Substance
©2008

Children please listen
To what I'm telling you
>   there's an evil force that can destroy
>   what you've been called to do.

Your salvation lies in the eyes
of Jesus, our King;
>   and the victory is in your faith,
>   not in your need.

People have tried everything
>   to fill the void in their lives,
>   something's lacking.

It can't be done by any means
that man can provide
>   you see the victory is in your faith,
>   not in your need.

Jesus knows all
and sees your destiny
>   if He met all your needs,
>   would you still believe?

For faith strengthens
the spiritual man
>   faith is God first,
>   and all else
>   He will add.

Listen to my plea saints of the Holy One
>   we have the victory
>   our battles have
>   already been won!

So just fight the good fight of faith,
>   and laugh at the enemy
>   knowing the victory
>   is in your faith,

Not in your need.

Created To Praise
©2006

Do you sometimes wonder
Why you are placed
       here on this earth?
Do you sometimes question
The reason for your birth?

Are you looking
       for a direction,
       which way to go?
Here's the most
       important thing
       you should know…

You are created to
       praise the Lord
       and show the world His glory,
Worship his name
       and bring life to His story.

You may be quite comfortable
In this life that you live;
All the fine possessions,
That some will never have.

You may be successful
Having houses and land,
But still, you must fulfill
God's perfect plan.

Lift the Name of Jesus
Tell of His extraordinary grace,
Do not be ashamed to tell someone,
You are created to praise!

You know the harvest is ripe
And the laborers are few,
So when you are created to praise,
Then praise is what you must do!

The Gift
©2017

I have heard the story
Of so long ago,
How Jesus was born
In a trough so low;
Not to diminish
Who He was or to become,
It was just his journey,
For our lives begun.

From the womb of a virgin
Born was He,
Not an ordinary man
But a unique seed;
Sown through the Holy Spirit
As only purpose could portray,
Gifted by the Heavenly Father
Who gave His Son away!

This Child of God's destiny,
Was to bear all the sins of the world,
Be crucified- but rise again,
For the salvation of every boy and girl!
His name is Wonderful Counselor
The Everlasting Father,
And Prince of Peace
To all who reverence our faith's author.

Yes, Jesus was born
In this earthly flesh,
So He could show me how
To live life ever blessed,
And how to overcome the enemy,
His birth, just another sign
Of how much God loves me!

Such a humble servant
Sent as our guide
The true depiction of The Lamb,
In my heart, please abide.
You see the real gift of this season you are living
Is embracing the gift that keeps on giving!

Remember...
©2017

Why do we take communion? What does it really mean?
If I wear white on 1st Sunday's, doesn't that make my heart clean?
I try very hard to do what's right though sometimes I fall very short
But I've always heard, "God knows my heart."
So a little sliding back now and then surely can't hurt!

But then it happened… I visited a church
And this lady approached me there.
She greeted me with such love and genuine kindness
I could feel myself withdraw and stare.
She joyfully worshipped and praised through song
Her movements contagious with glee
I can't even explain what I saw
When she prayed for Jesus to meet the need.

You see, there was bread on the table
And a little bit of wine, I thought *hmmm a snack-*
It couldn't have come at a better time!

But she prayed so relentlessly,
I quickly turned my thoughts
Listening now intently
On what was the actual cost.

She went on to say how we must remember God's sacrifice
He gave up His only Son that we might have eternal life.
Jesus' journey was not a beach vacation at a high-end resort
But the life of a humble servant who was killed for our story.
A Lil' bit of bread…His body was broken for us
A Lil' sip of wine… The blood poured from His side
Repent for your wrong and remember what He's done!
So when you take communion, you are AT-ONE with the Son!

As I wiped my tears and composed myself
I understand now, Lord, what you say.
It's not the outside you're concerned about,
But the nature of the heart is what weighs.
Your Spirit gives us an aroma
That is transferred like the mornings' dew,
So remember to check your heart meter
Before communion, you do!

Book V

Just Breathe ...

The reality is- life will continue to pursue and challenge us on various levels; but it is our response to those challenges that inevitably imprint Courage, Character and Integrity into our psyche!

-joybelle

Willow Wishes
©2005

Butterflies begin
From having
been another,
As a child is born
from a nurtured seed
In the womb of its mother.

But how many times
have you wished
You were someone
other than who you are?

Yet who's to say
That if all
were uncovered
You would like
what you see?
You can only be you-
And I can only be me.

How many times
have you wished
To be in
other spaces,
other times
and places?

Yet who's to say
with unfamiliar faces
You could
any more be
Loving the you
that you see?
You can only be you
And I can only be me.

Who Knew?
©2017

Who knew?
>   this white chocolate gem
>   could stir up a batch
>   of wit…
>>   maybe you thought
>>   but you didn't
>>   think.

Who knew?
>   this honey-laced pecan
>   could knead words
>>   like dough…
>>   maybe you heard
>>   but yet you didn't
>>   listen.

Who knew?
>   this melodious dew
>   could paint
>   such vivid dreams aloud…
>>   maybe you saw
>>   but yet you chose
>>   not to see.

Who knew?
>   You.
>   And even within the clutches
>   Of a symphony
>>   of negativity…
>>   I now see
>>   us three.
>   Me,
>   myself
>   and I.

Who knew?
Who cares-
Because now
I do.

The Never-Ending Nightmare
(The Story of a Captured African)
©2002

The floorboards squeaked as the dark-haired gentleman hurried to the cellar door. It had been almost seven months since he was captured by the lagoon near his hut in East Africa.

Where was he now? He didn't know, nor did he care at the present moment. Freedom was his only focus.

So far, so good. No guards in sight. No guns are visible. Wait– did I see someone or something?! No. Paranoia is setting in. But wait... I know I heard chains or something moving behind me. The beating of the war drums in my ears seemed to overtake my concentration. My legs felt like stiff bamboo shoots dragging in thick mud.

A shadow darted behind mine in the darkness. *What should I do? I had no weapons. Quick...think. Yes, that's it! It's the only thing I can do to save myself.* Without a sound, I ducked behind a huge boulder and hid in its cleft. Although my presence was concealed, my scent was still fresh enough to send the Rovers howling for days.
I remained still for what seemed a thousand years, and finally, on the sixth dawn, I viewed such a land I knew milk and honey flowed through its valleys. The brook that lay beside me had such beautiful pastures; it was as though my experiences were that of a past life. *Ah, such a relief...peace...freedom.* As I gaze up in the sky, an eagle perched on its nest and cawed–

Suddenly the trance is broken...I am squatting in the 9'x 9' cell with shackles binding my ankles and chains piercing the flesh on my wrists. In the distance, there was nothing to see but darkness. Will this nightmare ever end?

Dual Reality
©2020

There is no way to look and see clearly,
If the lens through which you view is tainted.
Until you can confront the holes and cracks,
Your perspective will remain a distorted painting-
As you frequently fill it with whatever is handy and holds,
Until finally, the dam bursts, and your dual reality is exposed!

Color
©2005

Black is not broad-nosed nor full-lipped,
        curvaceous, nappy-haired, or illiterate.
White is not blonde-haired nor blue-eyed
        educated or always right.
Red is not braided haired nor heavily wrinkled,
        painted, feathered, or beaded like a symbol.
Yellow is not almond-eyed nor straight-haired,
        petite, full-faced, or skin fine and fair.

Black is black…
        as the night falls after the day,
White is white…
        as the snow covers a northern bay;
Red is red…
        as the blood in our veins,
Yellow is yellow…
        as the sun that chases away the rain.

Color is a costume that lasts a lifetime.

Just A Dream
©2004

Stop. Listen.
Voices in the distance.
*Shh-sh…*I can't hear what they're saying.
Something about eternity.
Oh, that's silly…keep walking.
THUD.

A body of a young girl was found today.
She was in her bed and appeared to have died in her sleep.
But there's one thing that is still puzzling the Police.
The victims' hand appeared to be in a paralyzed position,
As if grabbing for an object just out of its reach.
Only one item rested on the night table-
The Holy Bible.

Racism
©2002

Why is-
      the sky brown?
What makes
      the trees blue?
How did this
trodden ground
      become purple?

Then I-
      pulled off
      my glasses
      of reality.

The sky is-
      indeed brown,
the trees
      are blue,
and the ground
      is purple.
      Can't you see?

Why is-
      black heavy?
What makes-
      white light?
How does
      the balance
      become yellow?

Then...
      I stepped into
      the sea
      of reality.

I realized-
      you can't see,
      and you
      won't see-

Until...
      you're blind.

Check & Balances
©2006

Who do you think I am?
> Perhaps that naïve little girl from many moons ago
> Seemingly shy, yet surprisingly giddy with such a radiant glow
> Not so ugly, but not too cute;
> With swerves of curves and locks to match
> Didn't your mom ever tell you big things come in small packages?
> Or maybe your wonder is if I wonder what you're really up to?

What do you think you know?
> Perhaps that I don't dream or have aspirations
> After all, what do I know about the art of frustration?
> Not so ignorant, but not too smart or rude;
> Such an air of confidence, definitely conceited,
> Ole' goody-goody church gal, square as the bleachers.
> Or maybe your wonder is if I wonder what you're really up to?

Why do you think I exist?
> Perhaps to be the giver of all things pleasurable by design
> Perhaps to serve with such vigor, one's heart can only sigh.
> To be loyal, meek, and humble too;
> To cook them mustard 'n collards, tater salad, and yams
> Washin', foldin', and pressin' fabrics, not necessarily excluded to pants!
> Or maybe your wonder is if I wonder what you're really up to?

Where do you think I belong?
> Perhaps a couple of paces behind, or just across the street
> Never quite side-by-side or face to face shall our eyes meet.
> I belong to you, yet I belong to me too;
> Within the four walls of common-law, not yielding to the wiles of success
> A basic underachiever, not ever worthy of mediocrity as its best.
> Or maybe your wonder is if I wonder what you're really up to?

Hmm- I wonder?
No, I don't, nor do I even care.
Because whether or not you wonder about me,
It does not cause my heart to either break or skip a beat!

I am who I am because my world view balances what I do.
I know what I know because of the experiences I've come through,
I simply exist to praise him with Character and Integrity,
I belong to him because he is the lover of my soul and the giver of life's tree!

The Sum of Who, What & Why I Am= *God (which is where I always want to be)*

My Glass Is ½ Full
Not ½ Empty
©2002

The beauty is in me, can't you see?

You say mole- an ugly disfigurement
    I say, *Beauty Mark*,
      the signature of perfection signed by the Creator.

You say black- as a negative, bad or dirty thing
    I say, *Ebony*,
      powerful and awesome the essence of a Queen!

You say 'black hair'- as if inferior and tied to a slave
    I say *All Natural*
      such locks hold unlimited variations of expressions!

You say fat- because my bones don't show
    I say *Healthy*,
      voluptuous and curvaceous head to toe!

You say ugly- because I don't look like you
    I say *Beautiful*,
      because I'm a unique creation that's phenomenal too.

You say poor- as if name brands define me
    I say *Rich*,
      I am my Father's child, and He owns everything!

So at the end of the day
I look in the mirror and say
My glass is ½ full, not ½ empty-

So really…
What do you see?
Not me!

Listen To Him
©2002

Where are the signs that show me the right way?
Who are the people I can trust from day today?
Someone said, "It's right here in this little book;
The one that says, the Holy Bible, take a look."

Hmm. How can a little book help me out?
These are real-life situations I'm talking about.
What I need is someone I can talk to,
Someone who will listen and do what I want them to do!

But someone said, "All you need is Jesus.
The only one who can help you get unstuck.
You don't have to beg, and you don't have to plead;
Just believe in Him, and He'll supply all your needs."

No one does that! Because nothing is free.
Doing what you ask is much too easy.
And we've all been to the same 'ole school...
'Nothing good comes easy'– so you're asking me to be a fool.

Someone replied, "No. I'm not asking you to act unwisely.
But to consider the possibilities from another side.
No one can duplicate the things I can do,
No one has the power I have to make you brand new!

Brand new, you say, as in a new car?
Or maybe you mean just a brand new start.
But that still doesn't explain-
No one can take an old life and start it over again?!

Someone said, "Try me, just this once.
You won't be sorry, and that's a promise."
I've lived my life, and I've done many things,
Sometimes I wish I could start over again!

So maybe just this once, I'll hear the words you say;
I've tried everything else, and I want to know the right way.
So speak to me now, Lord, through your Word today
I want to invite you into my heart to stay.
Thank you for allowing me the chance to receive
All the blessings that are mine just for the asking.

Signals
©2019

The pace today is a quick step, plus one
So don't waver when you see the gold
If you ever want to get ahead
You cannot afford to take it slow;
Gotta go, no time to entertain
Those who are slow to speak or are catty
I cannot rest for one minute
Though now sleep-deprived, I'm almost manic!
Why can't you understand,
I simply don't have the time
The more I run, the faster I must go
Complicating my focus- where are the signs?

Thus the cycle perpetuates itself, continuing into the abyss;
Until the scales fell from my eyes and I realized I was remiss,
In shirking my responsibility- I even abdicated my call
Not taking the time to count up the costs, I just plain ole' dumped it all-
On whoever passed by, whom I couldn't see fitting into my mold,
'How soon you forget,' God said, 'I first had to break your bowl!
Shattering that older man into oblivion, just to recreate you anew.
Why is there no grace and mercy for others when it was needed for you?
Did I leave you in the mire, born and shaped in iniquity's disdain?
Perhaps I discarded the one ounce of good that only I saw should remain.
No. None of these things did I ever do to my child
Even when you persecuted me
My unconditional love is yet undefiled.'

I repent.
Then I turned.

I'll stop going through life on green and pay attention to all your signals,
You said, 'To everything, there is a season,' this why my choices are pivotal.
Everyone needs someone, even though we are all unique;
The common thread humanity shares are God's marrow underneath.
So you can never, ever afford to cause another to fall,
Because just allowing them to stumble adds cracks to your pristine porcelain walls!
Life must be lived with balance, mediocrity, and perfection on each other's end;
I must press toward one while denying the other,
Doing all I can to help everyone on my journey to winning!

Restoration
©2009

When your highest hopes and dreams are shattered
And the circumstances that surround you fold,
In your heart and your mind, you've been here before-
Life can be so cold.

But it's not over- no, it's not over
Until the last breath is gone
There is still a chance to be revived
By the renewing of your mind

Condescending words and evil thoughts consume you
Lies and malice are present all day,
So many problems and trials to face on every hand
Peace never comes to stay.

No matter if disease wears you down
And your blood no longer flows
Just remember to completely trust is in Him
The source where all life can be restored!

Fancy-Free
©2017

It's not so easy to walk alone, to stand against adversity,
But when all has failed, and you're hanging on
Just remember, I am worthy!
With a loving voice, I'll speak to thee
With the morning dew, I'll show thee
How to love, how to be- just like me.

I love and care for you so much, each tear I'll wipe away,
Despite your past defeats, cast your cares on me today!
With my love, I'll keep thee
With my promises, I'll help thee
Learn to love, learn to be- just like me.

It's easy to walk like everyone, and it's fun to be fancy-free;
But to stay in 'the narrow-way' And show My love…
You must show them me.

Quiet Times
©2016

In the quiet times of the night
He holds me ever so tight,
He lets me know that I'm His own
And He will never leave my side.

In the quiet times of the day
He reassures that He's paved the way-
With His blood that was shed,
My debt was the price He paid.

I don't know why He loves me so much
It makes no sense at all;
To be salvation to the Prodigal Son,
A generation doomed to be lost.

Though in iniquity
I was born and shaped,
He looked beyond the worm that I am;
And saw me for whom
He and His Father created,
A unique and priceless gem!

In the still of nothingness,
the Creator spoke, and there was;
In Eden's Garden, in the dirt
He breathed life into humanity's nostrils;
On the hill of Golgotha, the earth stood still,
When He took the victory over death,
He silenced His will.

Ever making us His superior creation,
As we have the ability to choose;
Life or death, righteousness or sin
With our will, we must forever contend.

For, in the beginning, all was good
And to the dust, man must return;
No matter what end the spectrum goes to,
It's in the quiet times in which we learn.

Finding My Way
©2016

You said I'm unique, so where do I belong?
When my differences appear to be wrong?
How can I shine,
When it seems I'm forced to hide?
From the fire to the pit of hell,
Such agony and pain resembling a horrific tale.

What's the key for you to take the weight off of me?
There is so much to do
But no one wants to choose,
Only use me instead- just to get ahead.
Their thoughts on personal gain,
Promoting lies never minding the shame,
That seems to threaten the very breath I breathe?

The more I hurt, the clearer I see
But how is that possible when all I do is bleed?
There's no way I can be alone in this thing!

Who am I that I can't be tried?
Adjusting the focus of my spiritual eyes-
I must look a little closer.

'Though by the storms' tempest, you are tossed,
Your pain is not the cross;
Your shame is not the grave
Though you feel lost and afraid.

Your life can be simple and sweet
Just obey my words, and I will guide your feet-
No one else can undo,
The plans I have for you.

No, it will not be easy, popular, or pain-free,
You may not always understand; just trust me.
My resurrection power will sustain you in every valley-
For I am the Living bread!'

Inventory
©2019

Waking up seems so easy
As I blink the sleep away,
With each bat of my lashes
Death is kept at bay.
Through no mercies of my own
Or magical vices I could possess,
My breath slows as I swallow
And my heart beats within my chest.
I inhale…thank Jesus.
I exhale…thank you, Lord.
Today is another day's journey
I was not promised before;
To the heavens I pay homage
As I move my arms and stretch,
Sliding out from under the covers
On my knees, I land to connect-
With my Creator, my Master
The lover of my soul,
For its only because of Him
I have another chance to be bold.

You see, the other day I was timid
And a little too shy to say,
To someone who wanted to know
How did Jesus make a way?
What is so special about me?
Why did His love matter so much?
I wanted to say; it's not just me
But your life too He can touch.
He loves us all the same,
That's why he sent his son to die-
But I lost my nerve and said nothing,
The other day I didn't try.
So now within this moment
Where it's just you and I,
Help me to stand boldly for you
And your unconditional love within me abide!
Father, today, please let me lead
Someone who is lost to you,
So they too can live eternally
Now that heaven is in their view!

Wanting
©2020

There I go again, asking for it all
Never thankful for things both great and small
Continually thinking about what I lost
And what I must do to regain my footing, while I tallied the cost!
Oh, there I go wanting again, so much more than I could ever attain–
Then I remembered with God, all things are possible
My dreams and goals are wrapped up in His name.
All the times He's rescued me; wiped my tears, and set me free;
Never hesitating to shine his light,
Illuminating my soul, and every night!
I'm a miracle every day,
A living testament of his glory and how he made a way!

Here I go again, ever pressing on, no time to stress, fight, or be worn-
So, yes, I must always pray that I ever remain and never stray.
Then I hear God whisper, *Ask what you will, your heart's desire I will fill;*
Even though sometimes your way seems dark
You're a miracle, I can tell because I see your heart!
It seems like yesterday when we first met,
And you didn't believe your soul I could catch-
Worry, pain and bitterness had consumed you so
There didn't seem anywhere else for you to go.
One day you finally said yes to me,
And I heard your spirit ask, 'Is this what it's like to be free?
No bondage, no contention, no chaos or strife
I should have invited Jesus sooner into my life!'

How soon we forget what God has already done
His blood at calvary paid our debt- now the victory we've won.
Be careful not to fall into the enemy's snare
Of always wanting, but never spending time in prayer-
For the sin-sick souls of this world,
Putting your wants aside, so God's glory can be unfurled!

So here I am again, wanting to remain refreshed
That I might be a light to others in darkness.
Praying that my journey with all its ups and downs
Will help someone who is struggling to be found
When you plant a seed, the miracle will grow
For God provides the increase and blesses the overflow!

Trust
©2020

The days can seem so long
The nights darker still,
As I continue to press on
And remain in the center of His will.

Although people are all around,
It's as if I hear an echo in the room;
But when I checked in with my God
He said, "Your garden is being pruned.
The place you are in now
You've been in training for your entire life,
Each test, trial, and circumstance
Paid this position's brutal price!

Stop trying to compromise
And hold the old things, dear,
But grab ahold of the horns of the altar
And I'll relieve every one of your fears.
I know it seems complicated,
To step out and into the unknown;
But after all, I've already brought you through,
You know you are never alone!

You see, I remember all the tears
I counted them as they fell,
I placed them in my heavenly chamber;
Each vile so precious, its contents I'll never tell!

So when you look up and see
That your surroundings have changed,
Just make sure I'm ordering your steps
Because your destiny has been pre-ordained.
There is no secret to what I can to do
If you are merely willing, my child to be used."

My heart answers, Yes, Lord!
No matter what I see,
I stand secure in your calling
As I trust you, your blessings overtake me!

Distance
©2008

Wanting to be perfect, wanting to live right
Confused and torn by my fears, too blind to see Your light.
Asking for direction, not really wanting to go
The path you cleared, the moment was here
When You told me, I said, "No."

I know that you love me, I know that you care;
But sometimes it isn't enough to know, I need to feel your presence there.
I see the mighty works of your hands,
And sometimes I don't understand
How such a mighty God–
Such a redeeming God, such a sovereign God,
Could hold my heart in His hands?

Am I too late to find you? So many tormenting thoughts
It's been so long, and I'm sure you left me,
Now I believe I'm lost!
"No, my child, I love you, I never left your side,
My still small voice was muted because, within you, I did not abide
You also could not feel me because of your lack of faith.
There's no need to fret, just as in the beginning,
I said, 'It is good' when you, I created.

So remember this one thing, when it seems that you're alone
I will never leave you, so keep pushing toward my throne.
Do not be discouraged by the tests and trials
For they will surely come to ravage you more,
But don't worry, I allow this to happen
For these things, just strengthen your core.

Why would I expose you to these hardships?
So you can help someone else when they slip and fall
Shine the light on his glory
By helping them when they call;
You didn't run the distance to stay on the sidelines
So share your testimony of God's grace
Lend your hand in this hand-off
And help them in their race!"

Complete
©1998

Separated, consecrated, committed-
To the work of the Lord;
Rejuvenated, satisfied,
Because I have given my life,
Totally and completely over to Christ.

This Life is not mine.
This heart is not mine.
This soul is not mine.
These thoughts are not mine.

But the sins I carry,
           They are mine!
The burdens I bear,
           They are mine!
The cross, the crown
I was lost, now I am found.

I cannot come down
The work is too great,
I am trusting
And depending on you;
I am leaning on your promises
And believing your Word to be true!

Purify me.
Chasten me.
Humble my spirit.
Clean my heart.

Sanctify me.
Restore me.
This vessel wants to start...
Giving my life totally and completely
Back to Christ!

A Mile In His Shoes
©2017

Pain I know, hurt I know
Tears of despair all familiar;
Burdened down, shackle bound
These things too, I remember…

For I've walked before you
Suffering pain and agony
So know your walk is not in vain;
Just lean on me,
Mimic my steps for
My blood cleansed all guilty stains.

Mouths that lie, spying eyes
Spiteful words I know all too well;
Sleepless nights, hungry cries
Through all these things I've lived to tell…

For I've gone before you
Carrying the burdens of the world,
So you could live for eternity-
I, the Only-begotten Son
Gave His life just to set you free.

The Price:
>   To succumb to the whims of the flesh,
>   The wages of sin is always death
>   Vengeance is mine, and I will repay,
>   Cannot be your 'Manifesto'…
>   You've just gotten in God's way!
>
>   Narrow is the way,
>   And sometimes the path seems dark;
>   Yet you're free to choose
>   Who sits on the throne of your heart!
>   Whether you crawl, walk or sprint,
>   It only matters who endures in the end.

The Cost:
>   My Life & Your Pride

Thankful
©2017

Just a simple prayer of thanks to the One whom I adore,
The Creator, Savior, and above all, Sovereign Lord!
I am thankful for so much, both big and small
I could never say enough, for I cannot tell it all!

For waking me each morning,
With the clarity of mind and eyes that see,
Movement of healthy limbs as I stretch my arms to glory.
I stand on strong legs and move about with swift feet;
I have a body to bathe and ears to clean. I am so grateful to brush my teeth.

I am thankful for the aroma of coffee
I can smell as I start my day,
The bacon and eggs I can taste,
Reminiscent of the ways God has made!

Even the walls that surround me,
I am thankful for the shelter You provide;
To keep my loved ones safe
From the elements on the outside.

I am thankful for my heart,
That can give and feel love;
My family, just another blessing
God has sent me from above!

Even when someone I loved dearly
Is called home,
I am thankful, their life
Intertwined with my own;
I am grateful for the memories,
When the joy and laughter end;
I trust God will turn my sorrow
Into dancing again!

So as loved ones gather together
And enjoy our Thanksgiving feasts,
Let us not forget to Thank God First,
For allowing us not to miss a beat!

Book VI

Matters of the Heart

With every wisp of Love's melodious tune
Nature inclines its ear,
As Jasmine and Gardenia whisper their bloom
Intimacy lingers near.

-joybelle

A Mother's Love
©2011

As the sun bears the day
So the moon lights the way
To a love that's forever true;
And we'll forever be sure
That this love so pure
It begins and ends with you.

There could never be another
With the strength of a Mother,
Who could carry and nourish a seed;
With every passing day
A firm foundation carefully lay
As her body prepares to create a new being!

Everything she takes in
Is gobbled up and mimicked
No matter if it's good or bad;
You see, that's just the thing
Mothers are the gateway
Of generations and generations of baggage!

So when you accept this plight
Be aware you must fight
For the right to choose is a choice indeed,
But the real authority lies
In a woman who keeps her eyes
On the miracle and blessing, such a gift can be!

Oh love… sweet love
A heavenly angel you are,
From the jewels of creation
You fell from heaven's garden.
Sent to watch over me
And help me to grow
Meshed into your very existence,
Connected from the soul.
As each day draws nigh
Reality is crystal clear and cannot lie
That this bond is here to stay,
Forever it will be, just you and me
Together, hand in hand…always!

A Special Sister
©2005

Just to know I have a friend
That is there when I call,
Is all this sister needs
To boost me when I fall.

You've been there for me
In the storm, seeing me through my rain;
You've strengthened my resolve
To withstand the tempters' pain-
But through it all, you've been more of a sister,
As true and real as blood can be,
Sharing with me your wisdom
Of your personal life's journey.

Thank you for giving me love
Unconditional and overflowing,
Thank you for sharing your hope
Through the words of your testimony.

I'll always have a special place in my heart just for
you, Because I realize that by God's design
You were placed in my life for this particular time;
To season this anointed seed,
Pluck out the weeds,
And focus on the Masters' Ultimate Plan-
By cultivating all those gifts and talents
He's placed in my hands.

Your experiences and trials have taught you well
To teach me what you've learned,
I thank you for your candor
So now I'm able to discern-
What's good, honest, and honorable
What God wants for me
Is what I ultimately want for myself...
And that's just to be happy!

The benefit of you
Is what gives me joy,
And for letting me be me
This love will never be void.

Brother's Anonymous
©2020

What can I say about this hero?
He flies in to rescue his "Shero."
From yet another mishap and foiled adventure-
It never matters the cost
Or even if I'm lost
He's like a freight train running on adrenaline!

Two peas in a pod are we,
Plotting and scheming little bees
Exploring life's options out loud,
I never have to hide
My true intentions inside
He's always just standing, big and proud;
Readily accepting,
All that I can be
Supporting with a resounding, "Cool!'
Never manipulating
Controlling or perpetrating
Or selling me out for a fool!

It's hard to imagine another
Other than my Big Brother
That would genuinely care about how I feel inside,
But it takes that special bond
Connecting experiences of which we're fond
To brood a melting pot of superpowers, we can ride!

Off into the sunset…my Brother and I bumble
Into some mischief… can't learn to catch without a fumble
I lost my cape…he fashioned me another
I tripped over my life…he reminded me he's still just my Brother-

Never wanting the spotlight, it's true
Hiding behind walls, you can see through-
All because his focus is on helping others to smile
And for him- that makes his life worthwhile.

One and the same, all jokes in the game
It's my anonymous Brother,
From one 'Boot-mouth' to another!

Daddy Dimples
©2020

Give me an A…. Ah-hhh!
  As the vibrato breaks through
  The melodic sounds of passion peruse
  Each lyric of the gospel song;
  I stood tall and proud
  And hollered like a crowd…*dimple*
  With my Mary Jane's and Bobbie socks on.
  All the kids, we sang in tune,
  Although the words I used
  They were not the same- they didn't belong.
  You could not tell me this
  Because I made them fit
  My two-year-old understanding, not so strong-…*dimple*
Keep your eyes on me…some darted back and forth!
  I got so tickled looking at their faces
  The adults always tried to appear so sacred
  But would seem to do the opposite anyway;
  As if to provide
  Subliminal insight
  It's my voice, and I don't need your direction today!
If you can't follow, I'm sitting you down…
  They looked like pistons of an engine
  Ploop. One down. Ploop. Then ten…*dimple*
  I was laughing so hard at the view;
  I didn't notice it had gotten quiet
  And beside me stood Goliath
  Daddy Dimples had come to the rescue!
Everything's not funny…he said with a weak grin…*dimple*
  His voice said, "I know it looks funny…"
  His face said, "I'm gonna spank you, honey"-
  A constant difficulty this would become in my life;
  Discerning from within
  Not being moved by emotion
  Learning to master this skill was a fight.
Finally came the day when every song I heard was played
Instinctively I knew the right words,
It was as if Daddy Dimples was directing, and I was the choir, connecting
Those melodious harmonies together to be heard!

And the beat goes on…as discipline marches to the beat of its own drum!

White Boots
©2020

Once when I was a little girl, there were challenges I had to face,
I didn't understand how to jump- when up on my toes, I would raise.
Thinking I had jumped, when actually I never left the ground
I felt so very disheartened when others came around.
They found jumping easy and made sure I knew that they did,
It wasn't until I keep practicing that I finally jumped over a pen-
Then a pencil, and ruler too, I even graduated to a book
This lesson about perseverance deserves a second look!

I also recall being pigeon-toed; I tripped over everything in sight
There was nothing off limits- even air,
That would cause me to wipe out in flight!
I was clumsy as could be, but it never slowed me down,
I could run with the fastest, climb with the strongest
Yet and still, my face ate the ground.

Finally, the challenge became clear. I couldn't discern my right from my left.
No matter the tool they used to help, I couldn't grasp the concept.
I had these little white go-go boots, with zippers down the inseam-
Oh, how I loved my little white boots, a little girl's favorite dream!

It should have been easy to see right from left by the shape of the boot,
The zipper down the middle should have helped; it was just was another clue.
But I would inevitably put them on wrong, and it would frustrate my dad.
He would say, "Can't you feel they're on wrong? Can't you feel that?"
I always replied, "No, they don't hurt at all…they feel fantastic!"

Secretly I like the way the boots looked pointing in opposite directions,
To me, it added character, and they spoke my name with colorful affection!
Even after a while, my pigeon-toed effect seemed to miraculously fade
Could it be because those lovely boots had forced my feet straight?
So these little boots were made for walking, running, dancing too
Just because I didn't wear them, according to the norm
That doesn't mean the lesson couldn't change my view.
Although I finally learned the difference between my right and left,
I'm not so sure it was ever the cause of my daily snack from dirt's chef!

Daisy Indecision
©2007

Is your love real? Is your touch real?
Can your heartbeat I feel-
If it is real?

Is your love real? Is your smile real?
Can your passion for me be revealed-
If it is real?

Is your love real? Are you real?
Can the soul of you penetrate and fill-
If it is real?

The petals wonder…but the answer is in the clouds.
Is the conviction of a daisy enough to solidify doubt?

Pluck… he loves me
Pluck… he loves me, not
        Turn clockwise
Pluck… he loves me
Pluck… he loves me, not
        Turn clockwise
Pluck… is it real?

A Heart's Cry
©2003

Love is precious, and love is calm;
Love makes one's heart more treasured than a diamond.
Although all love is not loving at all,
But infatuation– at its most extraordinary call.
One must be wise when playing with the heart,
For many dangers arise from a misread part.
So please use caution and, above all– handle with care;
This delicate part of me that I choose to share.

My Heartbeat
©2007

Do I see you? Yes, I think I so
Through the mirror of my soul
This is what I know…

You're the one who touched my heart,
Without so much as a caress;
You're the one who made my smile,
Come from within my soul's treasure chest.

You're the one who didn't just hear me,
You listened to every word;
Unknowingly validating my very existence,
Giving value to my self-worth.
You're the one who was there,
Though you were hundreds of miles away;
Causing my thoughts to turn towards you
On any given day.

You're the one whose laughter is as genuine as gold,
Such medicine I've long desired in my heart of hearts and soul.
You're the one whose friendship
I've come to treasure and enjoy,
From the moment we first spoke
Our connection was like a fairy-tale story!

You're the one who cared enough just to let me be me;
And through these many gestures, your true heart, I can see. A
man who's kind and honest, caring and giving too,
A man not afraid to be the Best Man, as he presses through.
Not a man of generic gender,
But a replica of the original's best;
Full of Godly Character and Integrity
A Real Man, nonetheless!

So now that you see what I see,
Is my vision clear?
With the soul focused on God;
The matters of the heart you can hear.

Love Will
©2012

I love the way you view the world
On an axis
      so free and secure
I love the way you hold my heart
Like treasures of the Nile,
      so pure.

I love the quiet way about you,
As serene as
      a tropical sea;
I love the strength that hides behind
Calm waves
      of sweet humility.

I love to see each day,
As you see it-
      through your eyes;
I love to dream each night
Of true love
      by my side.

I love the thought of intrigue,
And I'm intrigued
      by the idea of love;
I love the feeling it gives me
And the possibilities
      that come from above!

I long to be loved and protected,
For the precious vessel
      and the gift I am;
I long to love that priest
For whom I will forever
      give my hand.

Love it what it is,
Loves tie binds all and seals,
Love has only one quest…
That is, Love Will.

Special Love
©2002

Time is standing still
The past no one can heal– but Jesus.
He can break through the barriers of sin
Tear down those walls of despair you're in
Uproot bitterness and guilt with His love
Let Him consume your very being from above.

Don't be discouraged
Heaven is in your view
Reach out and touch the Lord
His love will shine through;
In your darkest day,
He'll help you say
"Yes, Lord, I'll do what you want me to do."

Because my purpose is stronger
Than denying the prize,
I must fulfill that which
God has birthed in my life.
To give an account to You Father, one day
Is wrapped in my destiny and my walk, in Faith.

Yes, a closet Love
I once had
Small and feeble–
at its best just a FAD.
But through the fire
Now I have burst
Into another creation,
Still not yet perfect.

That once small thing
Has grown into an image
Of the Father above
Who is now ever-present
In situations and trials,
Troubles and pain
Our special love grows,
Because there's constant rain.

My Man
©2005

It can't be okay to forget the Love for which you've waited
So many passers' by, and some have even tried to be baited
But that one glistened Love, sat quietly against the road,
Watching, listening, and praying ever still, never again would the heart feel this hole.
It seems to grow with each passing day as memories of Love fade,
Tasks and business take its place; no longer does love have any space.

Time closes its eyes to Love and cries of uncertainty,
But you must be reminded- from which body's rib did the Master fashion me?
You see, the only for sure thing is the Master's Plan and Love
You can hang your heart on it; you can wear it like a glove.

But if by chance you get blinded by the enemy's dark cloud
Open up your heart and see a glimpse of True Love's vivid shroud:
Purple tranquility, Blue Heavens, and ever so Green seas!
Golden hope and Silver peace and an illustrious Red Love embracing!

But if you cannot see through the storm,
Around this Love, the rains will swarm
Consuming every bit of marrow that would cause this love to burrow
Far beneath this hardened ground of clay.
Searching for another soul of worth,
While emotionless oceans sink back into their waves
Yet again, giving birth to another.
True Love – No. There was only one.
But provide another full of passion and stability will the Son.

For my destiny was not to be denied; no qualities lost-
All my needs and wants to be fulfilled because I'm His, and He's paid the cost!
His gifts come without repentance or sorrow, so I can't settle for less;
Nor will I place my life in a precarious situation
Where I can never reap the Harvest of the Blessed.

Survive it… I will.
He created me and did it well
Can anything come out of a ruined place?
Oh yes! You'd better believe I still have His promises to tell!
So although my heart is broken, God will mend it again,
For I have chosen to walk with God the Father
My Friend, my Lover, and my Man.

Destiny
©2005

I know sometimes it's not easy
To all your burdens bear,
And very often you feel alone
Left within the Master's Care.

You know, it's only He who can
Comfort and restore.
But your heart still longs for the One
Whom He promised you'd love and adore.
The One who loves you-
Despite your faults and flaws, others see
The One who offers up prayers
To comfort and heal your body.
The One who holds your heart
And in exchange gives hers with joy
To love, cherish, and respect
Honor, trust, and adore.

I'm the One He's chosen
At this point in our lives,
To give you joy and fulfillment
To honor all of your heart's desires.

I'm blessed to be chosen
To be with a man with such heart,
Your love I'll never take for granted
Your side, I'll never part.

I'm confident in this one thing,
Of this, I'll stay forever true;
I was destined to be loved
And God knows I'm in love with you.

So remember when the scales seem unbalanced
And the words are as blue as the sea,
There's a deeper facet to this love
And it's fashioned be He who allows us to be-
In Him…
In love…
In grace…
In destiny.

Fulfillment
©2008

Learning to love again
Feeling a little like a child
Blushing at the very chance to see you
It makes my heart smile.

I've never heard such sugar and spice
Derived from the same brown jar;
With every sweet word so precise
And each nugget of wisdom a fiery dart.
Piercing through my walls of indecision
Breaking down the doors of inhibition
Melting the haze of low esteem
And giving birth to the
Fulfillment of a dream.

A dream only shared by two,
Honored by the One
Who sits in heavenly places,
Where all our dreams come.
When I toss and turn, I want you there
When I long for strong hands to caress, I just want you
When I need a shoulder to cry on, I want you there
When I long for your smile, I just want you.

If you can't see by now,
You're the only One I want to need.
Is it possible that my once frown,
Since introduced to loves' tonic
Has been freed?
Yes, indeed.
I'm free of sadness, free of pain
So free, I'll never go back again.
The past is long gone
The present is here
But the future is…
Ever brighter still,
Because of your love
In my mirror.

Second Chances
©2005

I'm so very glad
God sent you into my life!
You're a breath of fresh air
And have become my closest
And dearest friend.

It's nice to have that someone
Who is always there
When you're smiling or sad,
Able to listen to your heart's cry,
When you're grieving or just mad:
Has the ability to discern
When you need a good laugh,
But wise enough to know
When to pray and fast.

I often sit and wonder
If all of this is real…
Could this man I love so dearly
Actually my heart fill?
Can his love and adoration
Make my life complete,
Will the depth of his faith in God
Keep me on my knees?

I would venture to say "YES,"
To all of the above
For "I know" what God promised me,
Another chance at love
You're the original one he made
For me from the very start,
The one whose rib he took to fashion
The woman who hold his heart!

By purpose and design
I'll forever be in your eyes,
For our hearts are intertwined
Always.

A Good Man
©2005

For all that you are to me, and all that you do;
There are just not enough words to express my love for you.
For the Father that you are and Godly Man you've proven to be
I know I'm incredibly grateful to have you share in this journey
But I would be remiss if I did not honor your mother;
For without her love and guidance, you'd be 'just another brother.'
I'm thankful every day for this gracious blessing God has sent to me;
A Godly Man of Character, full of Wisdom and Integrity.
A Father whom I can always be proud of and confide in
Honor, Respect, Adore, Emulate, and have Pride in!
A Father who knows
God is where his strength comes from,
Who's not ashamed or afraid to cry,
And who knows to err is only human.

A Father who taught his daughters
How men should respect their vessel,
By first being an example himself
And treating her as a pure treasure.
Not giving in to her batty eyes or whines;
But together with their mother,
Provided balance and covered…
Daddy's Little Girls,
In the most strenuous of times!

A Father who guided his son
By the choices that he made,
Boundaries and standards and morals kept-
Not compromised for society's sake.
The life he lives with their mother,
Showing him true love, care, and respect
Is the only way God will lead a Brother,
To his destiny of the same…

A replica of the Original:
Not 'just a brother,'
But a Godly Father
With a Good Name!

Grateful
©2005

I am so grateful
For all that you do,
It's wrapped up in
The miracle of you;
That sparkle that seems
To glisten each day,
When your laugher brightens
My otherwise foggy way.

I am grateful
For all that you are,
A most precious gem
Sent from the stars;
To whisk me away
From all of my doubts,
You wove into my heart,
Love handpicked
From heaven's cloud.

I am grateful to you
For just letting me be…
All that I am-
          for his ultimate glory
All that I can give-
          'til it hurts inside
All I that I would live-
          because for you I would die
All those things of the past-
          present and to come
All will be united-
          and blessed with this union.

I am so grateful to you
For loving God first,
For in doing this great deed
No longer will we search;
For this consecrated and sacred love that is real
Whose core never ends,
Love is forever and deeper still.

A Love Letter
©2019

Dearest One:

All I've ever wanted
Since the very first day we met,
Was to be you're One and Only
And show you how good this love could get.

Each day I can't wait to hear you say,
How much you care and love me,
Then you lift your hands in worship
My heart races, and out pour the blessings!!

I love the sound of your voice as you talk to me,
It sets my day in motion;
As if you're in sync with my heartbeat,
My breath and all my emotions.

Who knew just a whisper of me from your lips
Could cause such life to revive your soul?
I did, for I am the Bread of Life
Whose hand you chose your future to hold.

I want so much for every dream
You've ever had to come true,
And watch you soar above expectations,
All the while loving and cherishing you.

Even in your darkest hour
I pray you would feel the warmth of my embrace,
And know my heart aches with pain
When you so desperately seek my face.

So though trials come to make you strong, I've equipped you with all you need,
My mission remains to protect you, My Love, As you continue on life's journey.
With every day that passes, we're better together. Your side I will never leave;
For true love has finally found its home, I Love You…for all eternity!

Daddy God

Book VII

Serenity

Vapor is all we are, gathering within the splices of time;
As the essence of our beings, like clocks, that you can never again rewind.

-joybelle

The Watcher
©2020

The eyes of our Father
So serene, so sweet,
Gently watch o'er us as we lay and sleep;
Wanting to caress our cares away,
Mending broken hearts, preparing the way.

As dawn ascends,
And twilight bids farewell,
He anxiously awaits our voice– no matter how frail.
For through the night under darkness' rigid sea,
Without His love and grace, comfort, or rest would ne'er be.

Reflection
©2020

After every breath, a new moment is created.
Between each sign, fresh thought is given;
Before each life, one is taken,
During each heartbeat, another has risen.

Home
©1989

My shoes are worn, my hair unkempt
My complexion mahogany
My wage, one cent.

My clothes are ragged, and my eyes can't see
My skin is wrinkled
My rent is a deed.

My children are gone, my spirit is weak
My only consolation…
Eternity.

After the Day...
©1989

As the day trickled like a morning's fresh dew upon the windowpane, the moons' glistening beams of light shone through an almost transparent figure that lay upon the desert sand.

The blackness of night settled atop her head in a great mass of fury. Great hills of knowledge and pervasiveness rested upon her rich mahogany cheeks. Her slightly parted lips ached of color and finesse, but did not lack the strength of a once vital soul.

With each fatal glance, every member of her body seemed to wistfully intertwine with the rugged and yet ever so subtle scenery. Her oversized lids lay like the serene, cultural plains of Zimbabwe, but her weed-like lashes offered battle and confusion.

Sudden arcs of shadowed moonlight protruded from the shredded sackcloth that showered her dark, sweet spirit as a cherished summer's rain in a desert land. Her long, scarred, bronze legs twinged with a final attempt to free themselves from bondage. Chained shackles. They were connected to a steel circular clamp that pretentiously hung like a millstone around her long, strife driven neck.

Slowly, the beams of light faded, and a new era of time was hatched. The confusion of the struggle weakened as the breath of a fresh day expanded into her being. 'You may have killed my body, but God has my spirit!' she whispered as she succumbed to her injuries, birthed at the hands of her perpetrator.

The blackness of night warmth the sun's fingers and deep, rigid shades of color offered the night for a sacrifice unto the day. She was finally home! Jehovah heard her cry.

Finally...
©1998

When the last breath is whispered
Death opens its hungry jaws
And captures what remains
Of reality.

Someday…
©2008

Someday soon
We will be together,
Better than ever
And better each moment.

Someday soon
We will touch the sky,
Listen to the stars
And sleep under the ocean's waves.

Someday soon
I will be with you
And never leave…

Death…
©1989

As her head turned, she caught a sudden glimpse of a figure darting in the shadows.
Her heart began to beat as an Indian war drum in her ears.
Slowly she turned around to confront it–

But wait! Was that a raven? A streak of lightning?
No… that's impossible!
What was going on? There couldn't possibly be a bird in this kitchen.
Concentrate…stop letting your mind wander…
What was I doing? Ah yes, I was making tea.

Another crash.
But the thought to turn and respond was never completed, as an unseen object
brought massive pressure to her head– then blackness.

Seas.
Water.
Where am I?
She opened her eyes to observe her surroundings…
There are none.

Soliloquy of Hope
©2019

Forgotten behind the cloak of these heavy lids I
 await the Bridegroom before I finally sleep,
Eyes that still dance, but my vision is now dim;
My cup is running over the saucer underneath.

You see, the outer fades quickly,
While the inner yet remains;
Take to heart, which part
You consume and allow your soul to stain.

Anthems and gospels still ring in my heart,
Their tunes reminiscent of the days of old
Such beautiful words to the Master
I will sing these melodies, 'til His face I behold!

Amazing Grace comforts me,
Now, It Is Well With My Soul
In the Morning When I Rise
God's Got It All In Control!

He's Preparing Me for that day,
By reminding me, I Was Created To Praise,
So When I See Jesus face to face
The Anthem, O Lord How Excellent, I will raise!

Nobody But Jesus has me Safe In His Arms,
Because He Lives, In Gilead, there is a Balm.
Like the Dew In the Morning,
He's Sweeter than the honeycomb;
Somebody Prayed For Me,
And now I'm Never Alone!

O How I Love Jesus- He's the Center of My Joy,
I Go To the Rock, for I Will always Trust In the Lord!
Swing Low Sweet Chariots and let me ride,
Peace Be Still…because on me
God Has Smiled!

My New Life
©2020

You think because my eyes are closed
I have left you all alone,
And you will never feel my warmth
As you gather together in your homes.

Please rest assured that although I'm not there,
In a physical body, you can touch;
All the things I have taught and lived,
Remain as a reminder of His love.

This journey was not about me at all,
But learning how to truly love God;
For in finding the Father, you'll realize-
That Life's ultimate power is in the potter's bond.

Do not fear my passing or the night,
As the days continue to linger on;
But busy yourself with God's plan for your life,
It's the only Sure Foundation.

You see all those years serving the Lord
When I offered Him my heart,
Was just a rehearsal for my new life
Of praise and worship of the Father!

There is no pain or sorrow here,
All sickness and heartache are gone;
From the time God called my number,
I dropped everything and ran into His arms!

I did not ask who else was there,
For it was Him I ultimately came to see-
The King of Glory in all His splendor,
And Creator of this unique masterpiece.

Death is not a scary place-
After all, you visit each time you sleep;
Its fingers touch your very breath
That escapes before you breathe.

But just in case you are not convinced,
I am alright with my destiny;
I am not with death but with my Savior,
Nestled in His bosom for eternity!

Transition
©2013

The house is now quiet, no movement in the yard
Sunday's paper is on the porch, and snow covers the car;
The trash can is full, and branches riddle the walkway,
Just a hint of warmth remains shrouded under a cloud of grey-
Soon enough without the light, the bleak and taut rope of loss;
Can chill any soul to the bone if we always live our life on pause.

Selfish by design are we to not celebrate when we go home,
Punishing ourselves and our God or the time He allows us to own.
Much like that house, I'm quiet now, and there are many miles on my clock,
Although you want me to stay here with you
My Daddy said, "Come child, with me walk."

It wasn't that my strength had waned, and I no longer held you, dear;
I followed my heart and tried to love through His reflection in the mirror.
Even when I missed the mark, He never gave up on me,
So I leave you all the knowledge of "Him."
My bags are packed, and my ticket ready.

Please don't chase and run after me
Your cries of sorrow may slow me down
When My Daddy says, "Okay, baby girl
Welcome home, Come and get your crown!
Walk these Heavenly streets of gold
Where your mansion is prepared…"
And just then I heard my name called
When The Lambs Book of Life was read.
I was ushered into the throne room
Where on my head was placed a crown
Jeweled with all my deeds and souls,
I was clothed in glory's white gown.
I'm singing melodious praises
To the Lord Jesus Christ who is King
In the choir full of angels,
As we worship from everlasting to everlasting!

You see, it's not black or white,
Yet it's abundantly clear
As life and death ricochet
We must die to live!

Ascension
©2017

When God called my name,
I did not hesitate;
For my life, I've lived to the fullest,
Sharing His mercy and grace.

I have stood in the gutter
And served those who had not,
I've even been to the palace
And I've seen things I could never have bought.

There is one defining thing
That continues to rest over my legacy,
It's the value of the one and only true God,
His Sovereignty as Master and Creator of me!

The only one who's kept me under His mighty wing,
While this pilgrimage I journey,
Fighting the good fight,
Thwarting the enemy's sting.

Many battles were fought along the way
But the war has already been won,
So take solace in this, my dear loved ones
Jesus died so he could welcome us, saying, Well Done!

Don't waste your days
Being angry or feeling sad,
For God's purpose for your life
It is for you to fully live out your dash.

From the time we're born,
Until the time we die;
God gives us the spaces in between,
To make the most of this life.

It comes with good and evil,
Fast and chaotic days and nights;
But there's never a need to worry
For God gives new mercies each day for this plight.

Life's stage constantly shifted
But I did not miss a beat,
Because of this race, I've run well
I'm finally home…for He's lifted me off my feet!

A Whisper
©2020

Sometimes I feel so overwhelmed, and I cannot settle my spirit
There are those days when everything I do
It seems to have a little hiccup.
Instead of honoring the frustration and bingeing on the nonsense;
I decided to take a more practical approach
And just *Whisper sweet nothings and promises!*
Sounds silly, Yes it does! But if you want to turn things around-
One day when chaos comes to your door
Whisper goodness, and watch your frown turn upside down!

Peace
©2002

Oh, what peace, incredible peace, I've finally found that sweet release!
Oh, what joy, such glorious joy- now that Your smile, my heart employs!

Spirit Moving
©2007

I'm on my way to that glorious city
On my way to that place called heaven
Where there's peace, love, joy, and happiness
I'm pressing toward the mark…just to make it!

I've been striving to be perfect- like Jesus, just like the Master
He took those burdens off my shoulders
I know I'm only a tattered vessel
But I'm clean and willing to be molded.

Every day and every night… Glory, glory, hallelujah
When things just aren't right… I can feel Your Spirit moving
Cleansing me, healing me, and giving me the strength I need
To continue praising your name forevermore
Jesus, you're the lamb I most adore.

Thanks
©2002

Daily I must die that He might live
      Within me.
Daily I must fight the wars of this world
      Around me;
      I will give my all to you
      I will be thankful unto you.

Just for the simple things that you've done
The blood that you shed when there was no one…

I know for sure that you'll never leave my side
With all that I must endure, I know I'll need you to guide
      Me through;
      I will give my all to you
      I will be thankful unto you.

Through the desert, the ocean, over the highest mountain peak
Your words I will speak in the depths of the valleys
      When the shadows are surrounding
      Your presence is with me.
      So I say, "thank you."

He's Coming Back
©2002

Watch what you do, watch what you say
You'd better get your heart right; for your sins, you'll pay
For Jesus Christ is coming back again

Don't be deceived, neither be denied
You are His chosen ones, the apple of His eye
Jesus Christ is coming back again.

Death has no sting, sting you have no grave
Grave you have no victory
For Jesus, Christ is coming back again!

In His Hands
©2003

For my Father is rich, in houses and land
And He holds the universe in His hand
With a whirl of His hand, He flung the stars into space
With precision and expertise, He hung the moon in its place.
With all power in His hands, He balanced the sun in the sky;
With love and perfection, His wiped tear rained the night.

From the dust, His hand made man in His image,
From man's rib, His hand made woman in His likeness.
From her womb, His hand brought forth the world's first Son,
From the sin of Cain, His hand banished the Adams' firstborn.

When all was lost, a perfect virgin did He find to abide within;
When no one could pay the cost, He was born in the flesh to carry our sin.
When the burden seemed unbearable, He carried our Cross and was crucified.
When the darkness of sin overtook the world, death had to bow to His Life.

There is Power, Conviction in His hand; there are Love and Salvation in His hand;
There are Joy and Fellowship in His hand; all you need is in His hand.

Declare His Glory
©2005

God made the darkness; He made the light
For any problem, the answer is Christ
Though persecuted, He gave His life
That I might declare His glory.

God made the mountains high, the valleys low
He's the Shepherd that keeps watching o'er the fold
His love is everlasting, and His blood covers all
Therefore I must declare His glory.

God made you and I that we might have a right
To the tree of life, He made the Son shine
All through the darkest of nights
Declare His glory, for He is worthy of all the praise
All my sins, He forgave,
And all my guilt and shame He erased.

Finalé
©2020

Listen, my children, to what I say
Even though you haven't yet passed this way,
Life can be challenging, cruel, and cold;
But you must remember whose hand your heart holds.

If it's the prince of this world, then you're in for a rude awakening,
His prize is what you can acquire each day you're living;
But your treasures cannot go beyond this realm,
The works of the flesh are tools that can cause the soul to be overwhelmed.

Mansions, exotic cars, furs, and magnanimous living;
Just some of the beautiful things he promises if you only yield to his bidding.
Your dreams are waiting to happen and are just a whisper away,
For a *fraction of the price*, the contract can be yours today
But listen closely and remember lovelies, don't be in a hurry to sign…
Remember to read the fine print, for your soul is on the line!
At first, you'll think everything is clear and oh so very great,
But this prince has a darker side that hides behind your lack of faith.
He hopes your greed, pride, and lusts are embedded deep within;
So addiction, perversion, abuse, and neglect he will also to you send-
And as these things take their course, ravaging the very essence of you,
The price that you paid, you found was too great, as he led you to your noose!

But take care, it doesn't have to end that way, you don't even have to wonder;
If you just allow Jesus, the Son of God, He'll satisfy your everlasting hunger.
There is no catch or special clause in a secret by-line, with invisible ink;
He's the Master, the Creator who knows everything you say and think.
He genuinely wants the best for you; he's a gentleman and will not force your hand-
So remember to open your heart to his still small voice,
And you will eat the good of the land!
He cares about your needs and wants, and even your biggest dreams;
After all, who do you think gave them to you, he literally sacrificed everything:
That you might have a fruitful life and experience His unconditional Love;
That you might gain eternal life, to live with Him in the heavens above.

So lovelies, I must leave you with this thought of undeniable hope,
Because of the life I lived, I've seen generations that couldn't cope.
Rest assured, I can say without a doubt that Jesus is my portion this day
And I can only hope that you saw something in my life that showed you his grace.
Jesus is the only answer…
In an eternity that's ever waiting…

Welcome
©2007

Oh, that I could give you love
Oh, to be what you're proud of
Oh, to soar on eagle's wings
        All I want is
        to be with Thee…

Oh, to dance so gracefully
Oh, to sing this melody
Oh, to praise your name so sweet
        All I want is
        to be with Thee…

Lord, I welcome You
With all, I have to give,
It may not seem much
But when yielded to Your touch;
It's more than enough for me.

Oh, that I could speak Your Word
Mend a broken heart,
With what they've heard;
Oh, to live with Majesty
        All I want is
        to be with Thee…

Welcome into this place,
        Shine Your Light
        and dwell in me;

Welcome into this broken vessel,
        Renew my mind
        and set me free.

Just to be in Your presence daily,
        All I want is
        to be like Thee!

Grace
©2017

How could I ever be worthy of your love,
Your suffering and pain?
When upon you my sins add many stripes
That thrash you again and again?

What did I do to deserve your forgiveness
Resting between your outstretched arms?
Turning my back on the One who loved me first,
As I chase the ruins of iniquities charms.

Why did you save this wretched soul
That was bound for hell's chamber?
Even after you conquered hell and the grave,
I crown you with unbelief and anger.

It's just who you are...
          the Giver of life's tree
          the Bearer of all my burdens,
          and Keeper of my peace.

Jesus, you are the Lover of my soul, in thy bosom, I will abide;
The Lifter of my head, the Comforter, will be my guide.

You are my Daddy God-
          the Matchless,
          Creator and Lord;
High and Lifted above all else-
          the Victor of the war!

You are my God of Grace,
Unmerited and free;
Carrying my unworthiness
On your glory, wings.

My filthy sins, you washed "white."
In the blood of the Lamb,
Receiving me back continually
With your nail, scarred hands.
Your grace and mercy have brought me through,
I am living at this moment because of you-
And Your Grace!

Book VIII
(Embedded Narrative Shorts)

Forever, For Always, For Love!

Who can explain the depths of the heart?
No matter what you attain…without love, you have nothing!

-joybelle

©2008

All alone, on a mountain top
Reminiscing over the trials endured, one takes stock...
In the journey and the entire scheme of life,
How it relates to others, and what is your plight?
Then there comes the point in everyone's life when it's time to count up the cost,
My time for reflection has reached its peak, and I've found I'm no longer lost.
Once bruised and broken, tattered and torn by situations I coddled close,
Afraid to rise above circumstances, consumed by fears and woes.
I found a place in the Almighty that I had never known before,
I nestled, rested, and feasted there, and with His virtues, I was restored.
Rejuvenated, reconciled, and released from all I had endured-
Not bitter, vindictive, or less of because...He alone had the cure.

The cure was a potion of brown honey-
Sweeter than any honeycomb from Heaven's Tree,
Its goodness tasted of purity and softness, yet firm and ample with seeds.
Each seed a separate gift- which was planted for a reason,
Now ripe and ready for picking, ready for the harvest of this season.
There was nectar within each seed, a genuine marrow for my bones
It mended together wounds and hurts that had crippled and left me alone.
Those things I thought would follow me forever, or I'd take them to the grave-
This potion magically lifted the shame and made me feel safe.

How ironic is it this potion arrived as famous stories have told,
Remember the war that was fought and won at the battle of TROY long ago?
The strength and vigor it took to be the carrier of such precious cargo sought,
For so long its pleasure evaded me, so long its substance lost.
But true to the valiant knight you are, you rushed to my side;
Handed me the cure and said, "My love, with me whilst thou abide?
I'll forsake all others, my Nubian Queen, just to betrothed to thee
I'll forever be faithful and love you always... for thou God hast promised me.
Let not thy lip quiver, nor shed a tear for things thou'st lost along the way;
With my Lord as our guide, I'll forever thee hide in my heart 'til my dying day.
Only this I beseech thee, my love,
If thou wilt have me... will it be enough?"

"Oh my Prince, please listen closely to each word that springeth from my lips,
With all my heart I doeth adore thee, for you alone hast ported this lost ship.
I'd take none other's hand in mine and promise to be true,
To honor and respect thee, my Lord hast betrothed me to.
As the sun shines above the earth, and the moon lights the midnight sky;
God hast heard my prayers of the heart and seen fit to join me to thy side.
Because my Knight, of this one truth you'll forever be enough
Only my Lord has knitted us together… and only for you doeth my heart rush.
So fear not, my love, I accept thine hand and willingly with thee I will go
For the shackles loosed by thine loving heart, will forever your love for me show."

Realizing the potion had taken effect, a moment was not to be lost;
For the substance of a worthy vessel is wrapped up in its cost.
Time and experience has taught me well to be honest with myself,
Continuing a life full of masquerades is not worth Solomon's wealth.
So how could my cost be too great? Why would naïve lips lie?
If the prize of being His faithful servant is to be blessed with being by your side?
You're more than I ever hoped for, and worth more than gold to me;
You're my Knight in Shining Armor,
You're my Fairy Tale
Beginning and Ending!

Pause
Next Reading

My Love's Design

©2008

The Father fashioned you
With care and expertise,
Tried in the fire-
Tested beyond belief.

Those nostrils created,
Within whom He breathed life;
From the same which he extracted,
That unique rib from which came I.

Just a fragile piece of you,
Not whole, but in part as designed;
Without its other counterparts,
Life would surely be denied.

Qualities that enhance your own
Is what I have within,
Emotions, sentiment, and passion-
Create a dual existence.

A diamond in the rough
First coal, now precious and pure,
Set apart just for me-
Because Love endured.

Through space and time Love's purpose
And master plan was set in motion,
Its full intent masked
By traps of past devotions.

But when the surrender was inevitable
Surrender to Love's Design did we,
Now we find our hearts cannot hold
Such passion this key has freed.

We sail above the clouds
Piercing through turbulent tribulations,
Our Love standing the test of time,
No matter the situation.

How is it that two so different, can be the same?
Interlocked so profusely, neither can refrain…
From loving, caring, and trusting unconditionally
Nothing ever too sacred to tell, no secret too silent to keep?
No word ever uttered that would mangle the heart,
No deed done with intent upon firing a deceitful dart?
But always feeling the hurts and pains
That seek to crush each other,
With Love, we've gained
We stand ready to defend one another.
With you in me and I in you
We are one forever in Him
Bound by that blessed union
A three-chord harmony blend.

Love's Design was right all along
The pattern cut, the mold broken;
None to which is comparable,
To this union so full of devotion.

For you have found in me
And I in you, Our Treasure
Never again will we search
For Love Designed our cup full measure!

Pause
Next Reading

O How I Love Thee

©2008

O how I love thee
Let me count the ways,
O how much I adore thee
I think of you night and day.

O how I want
To make you proud of me,
To be the only one
For whom your heart beats.
O just to be
The apple of your eye,
To see your shining countenance
And feel your bursting pride!

O to have the honor
Of holding your heart,
And being the groomer and keeper
Of this most treasured part.
Without which emotion
Would shed no tear,
Without which hurt
Would have no fear.
Without which joy
Would have no pleasure,
Without which love
Would know no measure.

O how I love thee
In every moment that is mine,
Not withholding anything
No word, nor deed… nothing of any kind.

All that I have
Is yours for the asking,
And on my knees, I'll stay
Forever praying and fasting;
That our love will remain
Fresh, new, and surreal-
Spontaneous, free, and evolving
Into something, only our hearts would feel!

O how I love thee
In a simple way, I do;
Honoring and cherishing
The very presence of you.
O to give you my dreams
And the key to my secret world,
To open the door of my heart
And surrender my pearls...
Wherein lies the essence of Joy
With harmony that sings,
An intimate song of Love
That is never-ending.
Its ever-resounding tone
Tunes the beat of another drum,
Keeping our hearts intertwined
With each Love chord that is strum.

O how I love thee
And blessed am I this day,
That God chose me
To receive the love you freely gave.
Without reservation or hesitation,
Without condition or strings,
Guiding the ears of the listening But
using truth and honesty.
As a foundation to stand,
Being real and candid
Showed me the true man;
In which Character abides
Integrity and Morality too,
The fear of God and Sensitivity
And Intellectually Astute!

O how I love thee
Such a love I've never known,
It's as if my heart would burst from within
From such passion.
I'm thankful every day
God saw fit to give my miracle life,
He did this when you loved me
So we could experience His softer side.
The peace in living a blessed and fulfilled life,
The honor in giving a worthy and unadulterated sacrifice;
The comfort in feeling our destiny was more than fate,
The pleasure of knowing you're my one true love… my mate!

Pause
Next Reading

True Love

©2008

Just the sound of your voice sets my day in motion.
It's as if you're in sync with my heartbeat, my breath, and my emotions.
Who knew just a whisper from your lips could spin my life out of control?
Is that to say that I do not know whose hand I choose for my future to hold?
No. I am a woman who knows what she wants and deserves,
Not to be confused with those who've trampled hearts with ill-spoken words
Tainted with hatred, spite, mistrust, and deceit
These are not the secrets in my closet I must keep.

For my future is held upright by the one who spun the world into space,
He dangled the stars and hung the planets on a picture frame called the milky way.
That same man designed another, a replica to be exact;
To him, which my heart I gave, and together we made a pact.

Each day I can't wait to hear you say,
"Hey baby…call me" or "Do you know how much I love you?"
It's been so long since those words were reciprocated or registered any truth,
But I can honestly say without hesitation that through it all…I love you!
All I ever wanted since the very first day we met
Was to be forever your lady and learn how good this love could get.
I just wanted to be needed, just as I need you so
My prayer, O God, why such pain? Why is it in control?

'But it's not,' He told me, 'it's just a test
To strengthen your testimony-
To prove to others, I am God
No matter how discouraged they might be.

They'll look at you and remember
The days not long ago,
How I brought you out
And lifted the debt you owed.

So though trials come to make you strong
The test is often in the journey,
Hold your head up and keep the faith
Knowing I've already given you all you need.

The angels and prayers I send, will not stop because of the rain,
I know that our distance apart is not an easy thing;
Through sleet, floods, and snow
They'll go where ever I can't,
My mission is to protect you, my love,
With all that I am.

My heart aches with pain when you're going through,
I pray that the Father would send the Comforter to you-
As a guide and assurance that He will forever with you stay,
And all that comes to plague you would forever pass away.

When you cry, I cry
You never cry alone
When you're sad, I'm sad
Because without you, my house is no home.

Too many days have passed
When I could not be there for you,
The nights your body is torn with pain
And praying was all I knew to do.

But I believe that we'll make it and we're so much better together
Every day that passes presents a different type of weather;
But persevere the storm we have and will
No matter the shades of gray,
True love has found its home
And in my heart, it will stay.

I want so much for every dream
You've ever had to come true,
And spend the rest of my life
Loving and cherishing you.

If you only knew,
What I wouldn't give to see that blessed smile,
To know that these tests and trials are over and done
To celebrate the victory of a battle fought and won.

Know that I will never, ever leave your side
This season that we share was designed for us a lifetime.
I'll stand firm next to you, as long as you allow
No matter how strong the winds,
My feet are planted on solid ground.

Pause
Next Reading

Unconditional Love

©2008

So long I've waited for you
The one for whom my hearts beats,
To come into my life
And sweep me off my feet.

I've seen you in my dreams
Standing by my side,
Pushing me and upholding me,
While God your paths He guides.

You can see me like no other,
As a vessel for God first;
Confidently knowing that everything He put in me,
Only He can cause to be birthed.

You fervently pray for me
And lift our love and my gifts to the sky,
Always wanting God's best,
Your prayers cannot be denied.

You allow me to be the 'weaker vessel'
Just as God created me to be,
Emotional, passionate, and fun-loving
Spontaneous and full of glee!

But also highly intelligent
Skillful and creative too,
Very difficult to be defined
But honest, caring, and true.

A woman who's strong and knows it
But views Integrity as gold,
Full of Godly Character
And vows these standards to uphold.

You see the God within
And embrace it in its entirety,
Not changing or molding the pot
But cherishing and appreciating…
The fact that you're the One
           Chosen to hold such a treasure
And be the rightful heir
           To riches beyond measure.

Because you know where my heart belongs
God will sustain and push you too,
For just as He's purposed a destiny for my life
As the Priest, He's purposely designed a vision for you.

That vision will flourish
So long as you keep Him first,
Always looking to Him
And understanding what you're worth.

More than any earthly treasure could weigh,
More than you or or I could ever even say…

So this is why I come to you
As your partner, your friend, and your love;
Asking you to remember
The most important part, God is Love!

Remember where He brought you from
And how He brought you out,
Not focusing on pain of the trial
But on the strength and wisdom, you've gained because of the bout.

Remember all that He's done
And why He did what He did,
Because once you know what you're worth
You can persevere anything!

Remember what God requires of you
As the spiritual and natural leader,
And know-how necessary you are
To groom and protect this Dream Weaver.

Remember to take care
And spoil not your seeds,
For an account must be given
Of any and every deed.

Remember foremost
And above all the rest...
That God's Unconditional Love
Will forever keep us blessed!

Pause
Next Reading

My Promise To You

©2005

My love, I stand before you a woman realizing
God has placed you in my life as my Priest, and I recognize this.
I will not take for granted the gift of love He's given us,
And because of this, I promise to always give my all to you and ours.
I will cherish and respect you as the blessing that you are,
Sent by, He alone, who knew that you were who I needed to become that star-
That was preordained before the foundations of the world,
That same Godly woman that He fashioned, not an ordinary little girl.

I'll appreciate you always,
Letting you know each day,
How much I love all the facets of you,
The boy, the Man, the Priest, and sometimes even the Dude (smile)!
Knowing all these things intertwined
Make you the exquisite creature you are by design,
A replica of the Father
Whose heart and soul whispered through the breath of many waters.

I promise to seek God first in everything
As your wife, a mother, partner and friend-
That He may continue to mold me, to be the very best
That fulfills our destiny and passes the test!
I promise to give you and our marriage back to God,
Because only the Creator can cause,
His creation to bloom over and over again
Regardless of the seasons or if we're not sure we can.

I promise to remain faithful and true to you alone forever and ever;
To stand firmly by your side, through the good and stormy weather;
Whatever the obstacle, you can count on me;
To hold your hand as God steps in to set us both free;
To stay focused on this marriage and remember the victory is won,
Because our relationship is always more important than any situation.

I also promise to keep you, my Priest, lifted in prayer
That God will continue to lead and guide us as our burdens you share.
To be invited into your life during this space of time
I consider it a privilege, and the honor is all mine.

You brighten my days with laughter, which is such a treasure,
Your love has filled my heart beyond measure.
I thank you for just letting me be myself,
For seeing me and loving this artist on God's creative shelf.
Despite the many mistakes I've made, during a lifetime of search
Thank you for looking within…First,
So our love could be more profound still;
Not focusing on our past lives, or what we used to feel-
But understanding together, our divine destiny is wrapped up in His will.

Most of all, thank you for giving me back my song.
You've strum a chord the key of love, for which I've prayed and longed.
No one else has taken the time to be bold,
And discover what treasures this clam holds.
Only you can caress my heart as you do-
The mere thought of spending the rest of my life with you,
Brings tears of joy and anticipation, beyond what words could say;
Only you can make me complete in any and every way.

I thought I would never have a best friend,
A partner and lover that would stand until the end,
But God fashioned us to be together...
And for that, I'm grateful ...and we're forever tethered!

With every breath, I breathe...
Completely and infinitely.
I just want to grow old in grace with you...

The End

Just A Glimpse…

Simply Ordinary

Simply ordinary, but not ordinary by far
Complexity is my middle name; simplicity my blessed star.
High maintenance sister, yes that's me
But not in the fashion that's typical or ordinary:
Louis Vuitton, Platinum, and Black Diamonds are real nice,
Audi, BMW, and Mercedes, those yummy toys with a price-
All have qualities expensive tastes admire,
But necessary to make my heart leap…no, just things I desire.
Maybe a bouquet of a scent that reminds you of me,
Perhaps words from your heart expressed sincerely;
Surprised on a day celebrated "just because"
Always affectionate, and never withholding the various art of love.
You see, the prettiest flower blooms because God causes it to,
Words from your heart give me a little piece of you,
Spontaneous gestures prove a love secure;
An open heart is one of God's tools for being pure.
Purity in the form of knowing your mate,
That God has sent to you for this time and place,
Cherishing and honoring the person she is
But having the strength not to give up the mantel that He has placed within.
Knowing that she will be the very best that you give,
But also realizing she wants the best you live;
For she knows if both hearts are secure in God and each other's love,
God will bless this union, and it will be sanctioned from above.
Things are nice, but matters of the heart are more significant still-
Constantly availing our feelings keep a solid love real.
Reality is the duality we must daily live,
With our hopes and dreams of a future, we will give-
Wisdom, patience, knowledge, understanding, and faith
Back to God, who has blessed us with each other to stay.
The best for you is what my heart desires,
To please you in every way and set your heart on fire.

Not just the fire of passion that roars in your flesh,
But a constant rekindled anointed fire of a union forever blessed:
> *Blessed to lay hands over and anoint you every day*
> *Blessed to speak those encouraging words when I pray*
> *Blessed to fill every void left after God's reign*
> *Blessed to be the vessel to mold your seed and your name.*

Simply ordinary, but not ordinary by far
Complexity is my middle name; simplicity my blessed star.
Full of expectations and dreams of "we,"
Stepping on stones of the past, to boost me up to where I can see-
Where to go? How to get there from where we are now?
How not to make the same mistakes that I vowed?
Being careful to cherish and guard my heart,
For many dangers arise from a misread part.
I know you can never accomplish that which you cannot visualize,
Maybe that is why I choose to walk around with my spiritual eyes;
Continually asking God to show me those things that are not like Him,
So He can take them away, by the mere touch of the hem-
Of His garment that can relieve any and every ailment
Even toils of the heart and mind, Jesus' garment gives fulfillment.
I long in my deepest dreams to be serenaded from the heart,
The ballads of true love found though we're still apart.
A melody made just for me and given without hesitancy,
Feeling the love with every note, sharing in the key of intimacy.
Our love for music that we share is unique in more ways than one,
Music is the gateway to the soul from which this rib was formed.
So no, I don't find it odd that we fit together like hands in a glove
I'm much more appreciative to God for this blessing of love.

Simply ordinary, but not ordinary by far
Complexity is my middle name; simplicity my blessed star.
So you see, although I'm simply ordinary
I'm most definitely peculiar,
For that's the way the Master designed me, Petite and full of humor.
Laughter, I've come to know him as a close and personal friend-
I've drunk of his healing waters and drowned my sorrows therein;
He's been my constant companion through the good and bad,
My mask throughout this journey; the façade of a happier lass.
Happy, just in the general terms, not blissfully by any means
Until the mask was removed and beneath such torment took wings-
And flew to my Master, on a wing of a prayer nestled in the clouds,
His answer was swift and magical, covering my doubts like a shroud.

To ask of Him, why? Or maybe even ask why me?
It seems petty and of no consequence because the maker is He.
Only He knows what I need and what I truly desire,
Only He can fill my soul with those things His love requires-
To be made whole and sure again of just what my purpose is to be,
To know beyond a doubt that He loved making me,
The person that I am today, simply ordinary
Complex in every facet and fiber of my being.
What I've learned is this...my best asset is the giving of joy
It's something that I do freely, without accolades or rewards.
But what I offer you is far greater still,
Because your love has engulfed my heart and challenged my very will.

    I give to you my hurts, my sorrows, and my pains
    I give to you my security, my selfishness, and my blame
    I give to you my secrets, my closets of disdain and degradation
    I give to you my heartaches from years of manipulation.

Why give these things to you if they are what crippled me?
I gave them over to God first, and now I'll show you what I see.

    I see the hurt, sorrows, and pains cuddled in God's love
    I see the blame and selfishness, secured in His blood.
    I see the manipulated heart, dipped in the Holy Spirit's flame.
    I see all the secrets of disdain and degradation wrapped in His name

I also give to you my heart, so full of love and free
I give to you my body to satisfy your every fantasy
I give to you every wish that I have cast upon the stars
I give to you every blessing that has manifested in full or in part.
So although my heart belongs to God first and foremost,
I can give you all of me because He took the thorns from this budded rose.

    He gave me back my heart, whole and ready to love
    He gave me back mind, pure and peaceful as a dove
    He gave me back my soul, and in that, I found Joy

And to you, I offer myself and vow to give you more and more of me,
As I evolve during life's miraculous and incredible journey,
I hope you'll keep me ever close to your heart and on bended knee.

Just know this, my love...
Should the Master require my presence before our time has come
I will forever count my blessings, for, in my life, you're one.
I'll always love and adore you and honor you for who you are
And who you helped me become, by just giving me your heart.

    My Priest, my lover, my encourager, and teacher
    My best friend, my partner, my spiritual leader;
    My soulmate and my blessed star, this is who you are...

ABOUT THE AUTHOR

Joy LaVern Osborne was born the youngest of three (her siblings are: Yolanda and Danny) to my brother, Danny Osborne, Sr. and Doris Britt Moorehead Osborne in Portland, Oregon. In the early 1970s, Danny and Doris were going through difficult times. Doris then asked my wife Gwendolyn and I to care for the children because she felt confident they would be in good hands. Doris would later pass, and we adopted Joy and her siblings with Danny Sr's permission. The one thing he asked me to do was to make sure we didn't "break the spirit" that he saw in Joy.

My wife and I quickly understood what he meant because Joy was unique in that when given directives, she did not seem to respond appropriately. A case in point: Gwen and I took the kids one evening to a hamburger stand for treats. They were kind of acting up, and in a gruff voice, I said something like, *"You guys have to settle down so we can order your burgers and ice cream."* Joy's countenance dropped, and she looked as if she was going to cry. I immediately took note of this and then asked my wife to watch how Joy responded. I then said in a sweet syrupy voice, *"When I get you home, Joy, I'm going to spank you!"* Joy just started giggling and became so ebullient. We learned that she did not respond to *"what"* you said, but rather *"how"* you said it. It was the tenor or the tone that guided her response. There was something deep within her little soul that carried over into her life as she would sing as she did her chores, her schoolwork, and even as she ate. We started calling her, "Joy Bell."

As Joy went through her childhood, she showed great flashes of creativity. One year Gwen's parents visited us from Texas, Joy read a story from one of her books to her Gigi (Joy had memorized the story), and when she finished, her granny said to her, "You didn't say 'The End,' to which Joy responded, 'This book didn't say that.'" Her teachers at school would tell us how she couldn't just draw a simple picture as directed but would always add her special touches. At church, where I served as Youth Pastor and Minister of Music, we had the children tell their favorite Bible stories, and Joy chose the call of Samuel by God. When she got to the part of the story where God called Samuel as he was sleeping, she cupped her little hands around her little mouth and piped out, "Sa-a-a-amuel," the whole church roared. She also had the innate ability to remember lyrics. All the songs the senior choir sang, though she was not a member, she could recall. In later years when the choir would gather for a reunion, I could always count on Joy to give me the words of a song we sang.

When Joy returned from college, she was the only one of our children, along with my wife, who continued to serve at the church we pastored. She threw all of her efforts into helping us in ministry. Her creative juices just surged as she wrote plays and directed them, sang and directed the choir, taught in Sunday School, and even found the time to draw and sketch portraits. In 1999 she formally answered the call to ministry and served as a servant first, allowing God to use her gifts to encourage, equip, and edify the kingdom. She embraced each challenge set before her with tenacity and "took no prisoners" when it came to obedience and being in right standing with God.

Accepting the call of God, Joy worked diligently in the areas of administration, music, youth, women, and leadership at various other ministries in the Houston metropolitan area. She started her own graphic design, printing & publishing company (J.O.Y. Inkz); and is an author, lyricist, playwright, songwriter, vocalist, and artist in her own right.

In February of 2017, the Holy Spirit led Joy to relocate to California, saying, *"there was work to do!"* While she heeded the call, more significant trials would stretch her faith; but God remained faithful and continued to whisper, *"It is necessary."* Joy's anointing has come at a very high price! After decades of pruning and pressing, her testimony of restoration is the fulfillment of Psalm 126:5-6 *"Those who sow in tears, will reap with songs of joy..."*. From the *crypt to the chateau- the oil is now ready to flow!* Joy has come full circle, counts her blessings, achieved her B.Th., and is currently pursuing her M.Th.

Joy has a genuine heart for service and embodies a true spirit of Excellence. She truly exemplifies the Scripture, "And whatsoever ye do, do it heartily, as to the Lord, and not unto man." (Colossians 3:23). In addition, Joy is the mother of three beautifully gifted children: Brenton, a singer, actor, dancer, an all-out-performer in New York; Bryson, a senior at Texas A&M in Kingsville (B.S. Kinesiology); and Braelyn, an aspiring authentic jazz singer, songwriter and proud U.S. Marine.

~ Bishop Louis & Gwendolyn Osborne